Malay Muslims

Malay Muslims

THE HISTORY AND CHALLENGE
OF RESURGENT ISLAM
IN SOUTHEAST ASIA

Robert Day McAmis

WILLIAM B. EERDMANS PUBLISHING COMPANY
GRAND RAPIDS, MICHIGAN / CAMBRIDGE, U.K.

Wm. B. Eerdmans Publishing Co.
255 Jefferson Ave. S.E., Grand Rapids, Michigan 49503 /
P.O. Box 163, Cambridge CB3 9PU U.K.

Printed in the United States of America

07 06 05 04 03 02   7 6 5 4 3 2 1

Library of Congress Cataloging-in-Publication Data

McAmis, Robert Day.
    Malay Muslims: The history and challenge of resurgent Islam in Southeast Asia /
Robert Day McAmis.
        p.   cm.
    Includes bibliographical references.
    ISBN 0-8028-4945-8 (pbk.: alk. paper)
    1. Islam — Asia, Southeastern — History.   2. Muslims — Malay Archipelago —
History.   3. Malays (Asian people) — Religion — History.   4. Islam — Relations —
Christianity.   5. Christianity and other religions — Islam.   I. Title.

BP63.A38.M43   2002
297′.09595′1 — dc21

                                                            2002023078

www.eerdmans.com

To my dear Malay Christian Wife

PATRONA "NONIE" ABAO McAMIS

who has demonstrated to me what it means to love

my Malay Muslim neighbor as I love myself.

As-salaamu 'alaikum!

Contents

The Home of the Malays is the Tropical Island World
of Southeast Asia — including the Malay Peninsula

Preface

I have written this book to share information about the little-known Malay Muslims of Southeast Asia, the largest ethnic community of Muslims in the entire Muslim world. My perspective is that of an American Lutheran missionary who has been a friend of Malay Christians and Malay Muslims since arriving in the Philippines in 1955. For twenty-five years, from 1962 until 1987, I lived with the Maranao Muslims of Mindanao in the beautiful Lake Lanao area.

In addition to extensive reading and research about Islam and the Church in Malay Southeast Asia, I have been able to visit in Indonesia, Singapore, and Malaysia. I pursued post-doctoral studies at the University of Chicago in Islamics and Southeast Asian Studies, and in 1967 wrote a doctoral dissertation on "The Characteristics of Islam in Southeast Asia." Although this was a groundbreaking effort at that time, many new articles and books concurring with my thesis have since been written by both Muslim and Christian Southeast Asian scholars.

In the 1970s and 1980s I was extensively involved in organizing, facilitating, and participating in Muslim-Christian dialogue, and in 1974 I co-edited a book on *Muslim Filipinos* with Dr. Peter G. Gowing. In the 1970s and 1980s I wrote several articles in scholarly journals on the history and present situation of Muslims in Southeast Asia. In the early 1990s, I had the opportunity to thoroughly research Islam and Southeast Asia in the Yale University Library. I was also fortunate in having access to the libraries at

Concordia Seminary, University of the Philippines, Mindanao State University, Xavier University, and the Gowing Memorial Research Center in Marawi City. Although the research was limited to work in English and thus lacked the insights that might have been gleaned from the literature in Arabic, Dutch, and Malay, I tried to explore material from the various viewpoints of Muslim and Christian scholars, and I was pleased to find many new articles and books in English written by Malay and other Asian scholars. May their numbers increase!

This is an attempt to present the history, characteristics, present situations, and future prospects of the Malay Muslims — including relations with Malay Christians — in a fair, factual, objective way that will be acceptable to and appreciated by Malay Muslims and Christians. It is my sincere hope that this book will be informative and useful not only in the disciplines of history, theology, Islamics, and missiology, but also to those majoring in political science, peace studies, cultural anthropology, and Southeast Asian development and economics. For those interested in more in-depth information, the Bibliography lists many works in all of these fields. Transliteration and explanation of Arabic and Malay words follow the pattern used by Muslims in the southern Philippines.

Since I entered the seminary in 1948, I have had a fervent desire to share the gospel of Jesus Christ with Muslims in an effective, attractive, peaceful manner. I have tried to do this by living with the Maranao Muslims and being their faithful friend, by translating portions of the Bible into the Maranao language, by broadcasting for twenty-two years a weekly radio program for all Muslims in the southern Philippines, by personal witness, and by acts of love and concern for all people. My faith in Jesus Christ who has reconciled me to God by his life, death, resurrection, and ascension is the most valuable treasure in my life. I invite Muslims to share their faith with me and to give me opportunity to share Christ with them by word and action.

I have served in Mindanao for over forty-four years, an experience that has greatly enriched my life. I pray that others may be guided to true faith and worship of the one true God who wants all people to be saved and come to the knowledge of the truth. *Al-hamdulillah! Soli Deo Gloria!*

ROBERT DAY MCAMIS, TH.D.

1   *Introduction*

A. Overview of the Muslim World Today

At the beginning of the twenty-first century of the Christian calendar and the continuation into the fifteenth century of the Islamic calendar, we learn that over half of the world's population of almost seven billion human beings belong to two monotheistic, Abrahamic faiths — Christianity and Islam.

Although Islam traces its beginning to 622 *Anno Domini* (A.D.) or O *Anno Hijra* (A.H.), presently it continues its relentless penetration and is rapidly growing in all parts of the world, including what for twenty centuries was considered the "Christian World."

In its first seven centuries Islam burst out of the Arabian desert and rapidly exploded to the East and the West. At the end of this period, Islam was established in a wide belt across North Africa, into the Middle East "Holy Land," and then across Asia until it reached its eastern extremity in what is now known as the southern Philippines.

The first seven centuries saw the "Golden Age of Islam," which began with the Umayyad Dynasty based in Damascus. This was followed by the fabulous Abbasid Dynasty based in Baghdad. During this period Islam was on a par with China in its amazing developments of art, science, education, agriculture, political structure, and military strategy. These remarkable accomplishments are little known or appreciated in the Western World, which was still in the "dark ages."

1

After the destructive Mongol invasion, beginning in the thirteenth century, three powerful, distinctive Islamic Empires arose to control much of Central Asia, Eastern Europe, and North Africa. These were the Ottoman Turkish Empire in Asia Minor, the Safavid (former Persian) Empire based in Iran, and the Mughal Empire based in India.

These seven centuries of growth and geographic expansion in the Islamic world were followed by seven centuries of decline during which Western European nations gained control of most of the world in a period of exploration and colonialism, led by Portugal and Spain and later followed by the British, Dutch, and French — the "Christian nations" of Western Europe — who extended their political control over much of North and South America, Africa, and Asia.

Many Muslim scholars believe now is the time for Islam, in its fifteenth century, to resume its march and change the world from *dar al-harb* (household of war) into *dar al-Islam* (household of Islam). At the same time, many Western scholars warn that "militant" Islam is going to replace Communism as the main threat to the free world. There are others who predict that the twenty-first century will be the Asian Century, during which the dominant influence will be the People's Republic of China.

A closer look at the Islamic world reveals that Islam is not a monolithic political or economic power in the world. Islam is a divided world with no realistic probability of organizing a united front against the rest of the world. There are many competing Islamic nations and ethnic groups, and social, economic, and religious divisions. Islam is like much of the Christian Church — divided into conservative, modernist, moderate, liberal, fundamentalist, and other labels that require a specific description for each group or division.

Most will agree that Islam has changed drastically in the years since World War II. Muslim countries have become independent. The establishment of the nation of Israel has concerned Muslims throughout the world. The "oil shock" of the 1970s brought oil-rich Arab Islamic nations to the headlines. The Iranian Islamic revolution, with its holding of American hostages for over a year, caught the world's attention. The Gulf War and the continuing crisis in Iraq are a constant reminder of Islamic activity. Western involvement in Bosnia and Kosovo in defense of Muslim rights, plus the anti-American activity of international Muslim terrorist groups, keep Islam in the headlines.

Increasing Muslim missionary activity throughout the world and the

Arabic names of prominent athletes in the United States convince us that Islam is growing in influence and numbers. Muslims are reported to be the fastest-growing religious group in North America, with Mosques and Islamic schools in most major cities in the United States and Canada. All of these developments are included under the banner of "Islamic Resurgence" or "Islamic Revival" or "Islamic Renewal." What will the fifteenth century of the Islamic calendar or the twenty-first century of the Christian calendar hold for Islam and the rest of the world? Will there be violent confrontation or peaceful competition between Islam and the West? Or will they work together for the elimination of injustice, poverty, and disease and join forces to resist the pervading influence of atheistic, postmodern materialism and secularism?

It is not our purpose to examine the history and current state of the entire Muslim world. There are many excellent books and reports available that warrant careful reading.[1] Our goal is to provide a useful and accurate account of the history, present situation, and prospects of a significant portion of the Muslim world — the Malay Muslims of Southeast Asia.

B. The Malays of Southeast Asia

Southeast Asia as a geographic region includes the nations of Myanmar (Burma), Thailand, Malaysia, Singapore, Vietnam, Cambodia, Laos, Indonesia, Brunei, and the Philippines. The entire area has a tropical climate. The food staples are rice and fish. In the early centuries of the Christian calendar, external influences were mainly from China and India. The basic social unit is the family, living in small villages and supported by agriculture. Women play a greater role in decision-making than they do in India or China. Social and political relations are more personal than legal. In former times, the strongest person became the local ruler in his generation. The entire social organization rested upon religion, personal relations, and traditions (Furnivall, 1941: 4-5; Hooker, 1983: 55).

The Malay race of Southeast Asia includes primarily the people of Malaysia, Indonesia, and the Philippines. These three countries will be the focus of this study, although the Malays are also found in southern Thailand

---

1. Roland E. Miller's *Muslim Friends* listed in the Bibliography is the best one-volume introduction to Islam that I have read.

and Brunei. The Malays are a distinct race with a history of 5,000 years (Funston, 1981: 165). In prehistoric times the Malays were daring sailors. Descendants of the Malay race can be found from Madagascar all the way to New Zealand and Formosa. The Malayo-Polynesian people still live in most of the South Pacific Islands.

There is an ancient Philippine folktale about the beginning of the Malay race. It seems that God was lonely and wanted human fellowship. So he decided to make humans from a batch of clay. In his first attempt, he did not leave the first batch in the oven long enough, and this half-baked group became the white race. The second batch was left in the oven too long and were overbaked, and this became the black race. On the third attempt, God knew how to control the oven so that this batch turned out just right — a beautiful golden brown — this became the Malay race.

A more scholarly version explains that the Malays are a subspecies of the Mongolian race who migrated from India around 1000 B.C. and from other parts of Asia during the prehistoric "Ice Age," when they may have walked over a land bridge into the Indonesian Archipelago (Lobinger, 1919: 58-64).

The Malays developed their own culture and language which varies among different geographic areas. Today, the Malays are the largest ethnic group in the Muslim world. They represent almost 20 percent of the entire Muslim population who are almost 20 percent of the entire world's population.[2] About 200 million Malay Muslims are found in Indonesia (the largest Muslim nation in the world), Malaysia, Brunei, southern Thailand, and the southern Philippines. It is interesting to note that the Malays also comprise the largest Christian Church in Asia — the Roman Catholic Church in the Republic of the Philippines — where 90 percent of the population of over 70 million are Christian. Also, the largest Protestant Church in Asia is found among the Malay Bataks of northern Sumatra in Indonesia. Thus, the Malays are the predominant group in the tropical island world of Southeast Asia.

2. According to the 1990 *Encyclopaedia Britannica,* the population in the year 2000 A.D. is estimated to be: (In thousands)

Indonesia	214,410	Muslims	186,322
Malaysia	21,500	Muslims	13,730
Philippines	74,555	Muslims	3,206
Total	310,465	Muslims	203,258
World	6,920,000	Muslims	1,335,560

C. The Island World of Southeast Asia

The Malay race occupies the Malayan Peninsula, the Indonesian Archipelago, and the Philippine Islands.[3] This area will receive our attention and interest as we focus on the Malay Muslims, their history, and the challenge of resurgent Islam in Southeast Asia. In the past this entire geographic area was referred to as Malaysia, the primary home of the brown-skinned Malay people. Today a better designation is "the island world of Southeast Asia," for while West Malaysia is joined to the continent of Asia by the Malay Peninsula, it is almost like an island in the archipelago joined only by a narrow isthmus. It is clear that by race and geography, West Malaysia belongs to the island world, while East Malaysia — consisting of the states of Sabah and Sarawak — is on the huge island of Borneo next to the independent, oil-rich nation of Brunei. Therefore, our main concerns for Malay Islam will be found in surveying the history and present situation in the three nations of Indonesia, Malaysia, and the Philippines. Here, there is a general similarity in language, culture, economics, and politics.

3. The fact is that there is a common feeling of solidarity among the Muslims of the Malay world where, after all, Islam is the predominant religion. Muslim Filipinos have a strong sense of this solidarity, and though numerically a minority in the Philippines they do not in any way suffer from a minority mentality. They are geographically concentrated in a homeland that is contiguous across shallow seas with the predominantly Muslim nations of Malaysia and Indonesia. They thus readily identify with the Muslim majority of the Southeast Asian island realm and naturally look to it for support (Gowing, 1982[b]: 19).

2 A History of Malay Islam

A. Pre-Islamic Influence in the Islands

While it is impossible, due to the lack of adequate reliable evidence, to state exactly how and when Islam arrived in the islands of Southeast Asia, it is possible to suggest the most probable method and date of arrival. There is a great difference of detailed opinion among various scholars, but thorough investigation reveals a degree of basic unanimity. This consensus divides the time of arrival of Islam in the islands into two major periods — before and after the thirteenth century.

The earliest, mythical reference to the arrival of the "true faith" in Southeast Asia comes from a Philippine Muslim legend that goes all the way back to the time of Noah. This legend tells of a man named Skander Jokanin who was on the ark with Noah. After the ark landed on Mount Ararat, Jokanin dreamed of uninhabited islands in the world. As a result of his dream, he visited the islands of Java and Celebes in present-day Indonesia, and Jolo in the southern Philippines. He then returned to Ararat and took a man and a woman to each of these places. In this manner the islands became populated (Hurley, 1936: 260-65).

In the early history of Southeast Asia, the first Indian settlements were established in the islands in the first century A.D. At this time Buddhism was spread among the people together with Indian culture. In the following centuries Indian influence increased in Southeast Asia. By 500 A.D. In-

7

dian culture had spread throughout the area together with Hindu religion and art. A conflict between Brahmanism and Buddhism in the area resulted in a composite religious situation with the cult of Vishnu, the Preserver, as the dominant theme.

In the seventh century the Buddhist-ruled Srivijaya Empire was established with its center located at Palembang in southern Sumatra. By 1180 A.D. this empire was at its height and exerted its influence over the area from Formosa to Ceylon. The Srivijaya Empire was followed by the Majapahit Empire in the fourteenth century. This was a Hindu-controlled, commercial empire encompassing Borneo, Sumatra, the Malayan Peninsula, and parts of the Philippines (Mahmud, 1960: 290-91; Bosquet, 1940: 30-31; Ahmad, 1980: 134-35; Soebantardjo, 1974: 439).

During this period Indian influence was also at its peak in the political, social, religious, and aesthetic life in the islands now known as the Philippines. Golden images of Hindu gods have been found on Mactan Island near Cebu City and in the province of Agusan in northeast Mindanao. Hindu influence was most strongly felt in the coastal areas and near large bodies of water from Luzon to Mindanao. The Majapahit Empire controlled Sulu, the region of Lake Lanao in Mindanao, and the vicinity of Manila Bay in Luzon (Beyer & De Vera, 1947: 28).[1]

The pre-Islamic period in Southeast Asia accounts for the Buddhist and Hindu influence in the islands. Geography shows why this influence was stronger in the western part of the archipelago than in the east. Hindu and Buddhist merchants and priests came to Malaya and Indonesia from India both before and after the birth of Christ. A mixture of Hinduism and Buddhism thus resulted, which blended with the animistic beliefs and practices of the masses (Mathews, 1944: 32; Winstedt, 1944: 186; Mutalib, 1990: 13).[2]

---

1. Sulu and Lanao are now the two main strongholds of Islam in the Philippines. Lake Lanao is of special interest to the study as the home of the writer and of the Maranao Muslims. Situated 2,200 feet above sea level, the lake is in the interior part of the western end of the island of Mindanao. The fact that the Spanish found strong Muslim settlements in the Manila Bay area is an indication that Islam was an immediate successor to Majapahit control also in these islands. Further investigation of these relationships would provide a fascinating historical study.

2. R. O. Winstedt, an English authority on Malayan culture, finds comparatively little Chinese influence in the Malay world; the predominant external influence is from India. He writes, "With a little exaggeration it has been said of Europe that it owes its theology,

A look at a map will show not only why Indian influences were felt in Southeast Asia, but also why visitors from other lands came in frequent contact with this area. The sea route to China from Arabia or India passes through this island world. The two main routes to China from the West were via the Malacca Straits between Sumatra and the Malay Peninsula and via the Sunda Straits between Java and Sumatra. A third route was through the Celebes Sea which brought ships in contact with the southern Philippines. Since ships depended on a favorable wind, it is clear why they sometimes sought shelter in one of the islands for a longer or shorter period of time while waiting for such a wind to speed them on their way. This also resulted in colonies of merchants in various islands. In addition to the China trade, there was the lucrative spice trade in the islands themselves. This led outsiders to seek influence in Southeast Asia in order to satisfy the European demand for spices.

In pre-Islamic times Persian merchants had already established regular trade with China. A Chinese record of 671 A.D. refers to the Persians as "Po-see" (Mahmud, 1960: 30; cf. O'Shaughnessy, 1967: 55). Also, long before Muhammad appeared in Arabia, some Arab merchants had established trade contacts with China. The Arab world is sometimes thought of only as a desert world where the camel is the chief means of transportation. But the Arabs of South Arabia were noted for being adventurous sailors. It was only natural for them to venture to India, Southeast Asia, and China before and after the time of Muhammad. Although Arab geographers make no mention of Arab settlements in Southeast Asia before the ninth century, Chinese records refer to an Arab settlement on the west coast of Sumatra in A.D. 674 (Arnold, 1913: 364; Sidjabat, 1965: 30; Schumann, 1974: 429, 430).[3]

---

its literature, and its science to Greece; with no greater exaggeration it may be said of the Malayan races that until the 19th century they owed everything to India: religions, a political system, medieval astrology and medicine, literature, arts and crafts." R. O. Winstedt, "Indian Influence in the Malay World," *Journal of the Royal Asiatic Society* (1944): 186.

3. Bernard Vlekke states that Odorico de Pordenone, a Franciscan, arrived in Indonesia only twenty years after the first penetration of Islam, but no attempt was made to remain and establish Christianity. Evidently this was one of the Portuguese missionaries en route to China (Vlekke, 1943: 80-85).

B. Early Islamic Influence

After Islam began in Arabia, Arab Muslim traders appeared in numbers in south China strong enough to capture Canton in 758 A.D. By the ninth century there were small communities of Muslim traders in various ports on the route between Arabia and China. There is no evidence of Arab settlements of large size in Indonesia at this time since most of the islands were not directly on the trade route to China (Hall, 1981: 176; O'Shaughnessy, 1967: 55-57; Ahmad, 1980: 135).

Muslim sailors ranged far and wide from the Persian Gulf and Red Sea ports. They traveled to India, Ceylon, Southeast Asia, and China in an easterly direction. It is not so generally recognized that they also sought markets and goods in such places as Sweden and Iceland (Lewis, 1960: 87). However, because they found conditions for trade much better in the East, Islam began to spread in that direction. The Arab settlers of East Africa, South India, and Indonesia were predominantly Hadramis from Southeast Arabia. They carried Islamic culture to China, the west coast of India, and later to Sumatra and Malacca (Mahmud, 1960: 4, 12; Hamid, 1983: 1-17).

After the death of Muhammad, the early period of Islamic expansion was under the Umayyad Dynasty at Damascus. This was a time of unrest and internal struggle for power. Such conditions were not conducive to trade with the Far East. Later, under the Abbasid rulers at Baghdad in the ninth and tenth centuries, trade with the Far East began to flourish. During this period the Chinese records describe trade with the Arabs and classified them as the richest foreigners. Enroute to China, these Arab traders made calls in various Southeast Asian ports. In later centuries they became more interested in the spices from these islands than the goods from China. With the fall of the Srivijaya Empire in Sumatra and the transfer of the center of power to Kadiri in Java, there was a power vacuum in the islands leaving only small, petty, local kingdoms (Tibbetts, 1957: 1-16; Van der Kroef, 1953: 302; Marrison, 1951: 33; Winstedt, 1920: 5, 6).[4]

An early record of Arab contact with Malaya and Indonesia is found in the middle of the ninth century in the writings of Arabic-Persian geogra-

---

4. Snouck Hurgronje, a Dutch Islamicist, suggests that the early Muslim missionaries to Southeast Asia came from both Gujarat and Malabar in South India. He maintains that it was only after the advent of the steamship that direct Arab influence became strong in the islands (1906).

phers, in which references are made to the Malay Peninsula and to Suma-tra. In 955 A.D. an Arab writer, Mas'udi, described the various spices avail-able in the islands (Hall, 1981: 51). Muslim traders also left evidence of their presence in Southeast Asia along the coast of the China Sea as early as A.D. 977 (Fatimi, 1963: 38). There is a gravestone near Surabaya in Eastern Java with an Arabic inscription which indicates that a Muslim princess was buried there in A.D. 1081 (Fatimi, 1963: 67). Another tombstone inscribed in Arabic near Gresik in Java is the earliest evidence of Muslims in that part of the islands. The date on the stone is near the beginning of the twelfth century. There is no evidence of the existence of Islam in this part of Java until four centuries later (Hall, 1981: 76).

In this period of early contacts with Islam, merchants from Arabia and India established semi-permanent settlements in Southeast Asia.

> These settlements were established solely for commercial reasons and it is doubtful if any Muslim missionary work was carried on. The rapid conversion of Southeast Asia during the 14th century was thought to be the work of zealous Indian converts although there can be no doubt that existence of Muslim settlements, some of two or three centuries stand-ing, did much to influence local populations and prepare the way for later proselytizing. (Tibbetts, 1957: 44)

Although Muslim merchants paved the way for Islam, the dedicated Muslim teachers who followed did much of the real work of persuasion and spreading of Islam in Southeast Asia (Fatimi, 1963: 87). Here there are differences of opinion as to motivation. Sir Thomas Arnold's treatment of the expansion of Islam contends that Muslim merchants came to the is-land world not to make a profit and not to establish themselves as superior, but primarily to present the teachings of Muhammad and to establish Is-lam (1913: 365, 366). However, Snouck Hurgronje expresses a contrary view:

> Those who sowed in the Far East the first seeds of Islam were no zealots prepared to sacrifice life and property for the holy cause, nor were they missionaries supported by funds raised in their native land. On the con-trary, these men came to seek their own worldly advantage, and the work of conversion was merely a secondary task. Later on, too, when millions had in this way been won over to Islam, it was the prospect of

making money and naught else that attracted hitherward so many teachers from India, Egypt, Mecca and Hadramaut. (1906: II, 278, 279)

The truth probably lies somewhere in between the two views stated above. No doubt there were different motives in different merchants and even mixed motives in some. In any case Muslim merchants who came to the tropical island world in the early Islamic period were instrumental in introducing Islam there. S. Q. Fatimi, a Muslim scholar, has suggested the following chronology for the history of Islam in the islands:

1st: Earliest contacts — from 674 A.D.
2nd: Islam obtains foothold in coastal towns — 878 A.D.
3rd: Islam begins achieving political power — 1204 A.D.
4th: Decline sets in — from 1511 A.D. (Fatimi, 1963: 69, 70)

C. Islamic Influence After the Thirteenth Century

A classical Malay history dates the coming of Islam to Sumatra precisely at 1204 A.D. The *Annals of Acheen* have this precise account of the introduction of Islam (Fatimi, 1963: 38):[5]

> On Friday the 1st of Ramadan in the year 601 of the flight of the Holy Prophet of God, Sultan Johan Shah came from the windward and converted the people of Acheen (Acheh) to the Mohammedan faith. He married the daughter of Baludri at Acheen and by her had a son, and died on Thursday, 1st of Rajab, 631 (1233 A.D.) after a reign of 30 years 11 months and 26 days and was succeeded by his son Sultan Ahmad.

In 1292 A.D. Marco Polo, on his return voyage from China, visited the northwestern Sumatran area now known as Perlak and reported that it had already been converted to Islam.

---

5. John Crawfurd, *History of the Indian Archipelago* (Edinburgh: A. Constable and Co., 1820), vol. 3, p. 207, gives the following dates for establishment of Islam among various peoples: 1204 A.D., the Achehnese; 1278 A.D., the Malays of Malacca; 1478 A.D., the Javanese; 1495 A.D., the Spice Islanders. Crawfurd was a British scholar who traveled widely throughout Southeast Asia in the early nineteenth century.

This kingdom, you must know, is so much frequented by Saracen merchants that they have converted the natives to the Law of Muhammad — I mean the townspeople only, for the hill people live for all the world like beasts and eat human flesh, as well as other kinds of flesh, clean or unclean. (Fatimi, 1963: 8; cf. Hooker, 1983: 4, 5)

This northern port of Perlak was still under Majapahit suzerainty when Marco Polo called there. He writes in his *Travels* that the spread of Islam was due to intermarriage between the Muslim merchants and local inhabitants, often with local rulers' families (Mahmud, 1960: 290, 291; Ahmad, 1980: 139, 140). This is the earliest reliable report of the conversion of the local population of Sumatra to Islam. Another famous world traveler, Ibn Battuta of Morocco, confirms the report of Marco Polo. In 1345 he visited the north Sumatran port of Pase and described the inhabitants as Muslims (Hooker, 1983: 4, 5). The area along the coast of Sumatra was converted to Islam by the latter half of the fourteenth century. Although there are isolated instances of Islamic influence, "there is little evidence suggesting the spread of Islam to the [Malay] Peninsula before the 15th century" (Hall, 1981: 176).

Although contacts with Arabian merchants are reported in the early decades of Islam, it was not until the thirteenth century that Islam gained a significant influence in Indonesia. The dominant type of Islam that spread to the Indies was of the Shafi'i branch of the Sunni school. The development that took place as it passed through India included Indian influences of toleration. Islam rapidly and easily gained followers due largely to its adaptability and tolerance. The main Muslim teachings were presented, but many of the old pre-Islamic beliefs and customs persisted. The Muslim settlers intermarried with the local population and became integrated with the local community. The Islamization of Indonesia was a very gradual process, beginning in the thirteenth century, gaining considerable momentum during the sixteenth, and in differing ways continuing until the present day (Rosen, 1965: 11).

World events in the Muslim heartlands and in Europe had their effects on the spread of Islam to Southeast Asia. After the fall of Baghdad to the Mongol forces in 1258, the overland trade route to India was disrupted. This led to an increase in the use of sea routes across the Indian Ocean and through the Malay Straits to China. When the Mongol rulers were subsequently converted to Islam, this gave new impetus to the expansion of Islam throughout Asia. The collapse of the Hindu-Javanese Empire of Majapahit left a power vacuum and abetted the spread of Islam in the islands (Van der Kroef, 1953: 302).[6] Local rulers were converted to Islam and through force and persuasion led their subjects to become Muslims. In this manner Islam spread through Sumatra, the Malay Peninsula, Borneo, the Sulu Archipelago, and western Mindanao in the Philippines. Java and Bali offered some resistance but, gradually, at least the towns in Java were converted to Islam (Cole, 1945: 23-28). J. C. van Leur writes of this period (1955: 138, 139):[7]

> A second imprint on Indonesian civilization was made by Islam. Islam was a missionary community in the early Christian sense, with every believer a potential missionary for spreading its doctrine. However, though it had already been present for centuries in the foreign colonies in the East — on the west coast of Sumatra *circa* 674, in China arriving along the sea route in the 7th century, in Java and farther India known from the tombstones dated for the years 1082 and 1039 — Islam began to exert wider influence only in the 14th century. . . . The expansion of the new religion did not result in any revolutions or any newly arrived for-

6. R. O. Winstedt, "The Advent of Muhammadanism in the Malay Peninsula and Archipelago," *The Journal of the Straits Branch of the Royal Asiatic Society* 77 (December 1917), reports Arab traders in Kedah in Sumatra in 915 A.D., but believes that Islam was not established there until the early fifteenth century according to the dates on the Arabic tombstones found in Sumatra and Java. Winstedt writes that in 1478 Muslim princes of Java combined to overthrow the Hindu empire of Majapahit. At that time a ruler named Demak reportedly proclaimed himself Sultan. Arnold, p. 2, adds, "When the Mongol hordes sacked Baghdad (A.D. 1258) and drowned in blood the faded glory of the Abbasid dynasty — when the Muslims were expelled from Cordova by Ferdinand of Leon and Castille (A.D. 1236) and Granada, the last stronghold of Islam in Spain, paid tribute to the Christian king — Islam had just gained a footing in the islands of the Malay Archipelago." John Rauws, et al., *The Netherland Indies* (London and New York: World Dominion Press, 1935), pp. 99-101.

7. R. L. Archer, "Muhammadan Mysticism in Sumatra," *Journal of the Malayan Branch of the Royal Asiatic Society* 15, no. 2 (1937). Archer doubts that Sumatra was converted to Islam between 1270 and 1275 as some suppose. He bases this on the fact that the tombstone of the reputed founder of Islam in the kingdom of Sumatra Pasai in Northern Sumatra bears the Muslim date of 1297 A.D. The introduction of Islam in Sumatra occurred in the early centuries of the Hijrah, when Arab traders established trading stations along the coasts on the route to China where there were large numbers of Arab traders.

eign colonists coming to power — the Indonesian regime did not undergo a single change due to it. It is not clear what the causes were that the great proselytization for the new gospel in Southeast Asia began only in the 13th century though it had already been known for centuries. Perhaps it was a repercussion of the Mongol wars and the threat to the Moslem caliphates; perhaps too more forceful counter-propaganda arose as a result of the coming of Christian missionaries during the rule of the Mongol khans. The expansion of Islam later gained strength through the eruption of the struggle with the Portuguese in Asia after which the Moslems consciously counteracted every Christian influence.

A description of the manner in which Islam became established in the islands is given by J. Rauws, a Dutch missionary to Indonesia.

In 1416 Atjeh (Acheh) and Deli, the northern part of Sumatra, were entirely won over for Islam, and from here it penetrated into regions beyond. About the year 1500 it reached Java. It was not a conquest by the sword, but peaceable propaganda by preaching and especially by the influence of social ascendancy. The leading part was played by merchants, who on their journeys had come in contact with Islam and adopted the tongue and the customs of the people among whom he trades, wins their hearts by marriage with the daughters of the land, makes an impression by his superior knowledge and civilization and by the purchase of slaves increases his own importance. The people among whom he labors become envious of his position and soon imitate him. (1911: 241)

There seems to be agreement in both Muslim and Christian sources that Muslims from India were instrumental in this spread of Islam in the islands. Stanley Karnow writes:

Indian Moslem merchants from Gujarat and Bengal also brought Islam to Southeast Asia, and the creed adapted itself to the new environment. It syncretized with earlier Brahmanism and Buddhism or fused with local mysticism, and it is an Islam that few Arabs would recognize. Except for the Darul Islam insurgents of Java and other fanatic bands elsewhere in Indonesia, most of whom agitate hopelessly for a theocratic state, Indonesian Moslems are tolerant, unorthodox and almost casual about religion. In Malaya as well, it appears more a formality than a fervent

faith . . . (1964: 12). The Indian Moslems — like the Hindus and Buddhists before them and the Europeans to follow — recognized the ad-
vantage of establishing themselves closer to their sources of raw materi-
als. They moved into the islands of Indonesia, and eventually they based
their firms in the conveniently located Malayan town of Malacca. (32)

Malacca thus became a trading center for Southeast Asia dominated by
Indian Muslims. It also became a center from which Islam spread to the local rulers in insular Southeast Asia. This spread of Islam preceded the European influence in this area (Karnow, 1964; O'Shaughnessy, 1967: 58, 59).

A Muslim historian, S. F. Mahmud, adds his views concerning the role
of the Indian Muslim merchants in the spread of Islam:

> The conversion of coastal Sumatra to Islam was really the work of Guja-
> rati and Bengali Muslim merchants. . . . Once the door of Southeast Asia
> had been opened to Islam, the religion spread with great rapidity. (1960:
> 281)

He explains that this was because all the foreign trade had been in the
hands of the Muslims for 600 years. Merchants had come from Arabia,
Persia, and India with goods from Europe which were traded for silks and
spices. Thus Islam made its first appearance in the Malayan Peninsula in
the fourteenth century. Malacca was the first state that became Muslim. It
was from Malacca that Islam continued its spread to the islands of Southeast Asia (Mahmud, 1960: 281).

The Malays along the coast were generally a seafaring people and were
the first to be converted to Islam. In the interior areas the animistic tribes
offered greater resistance to the intrusion of Islam. Therefore, it was the
seventeenth century before Islam gained a firm footing in the interior sections of Southeast Asia. There was one exception; a stronghold of Islam
developed in south-central Sumatra, near the west coast, among the
Minangkabao tribe which became entirely Muslim in the fifteenth century
(Simon, 1912: 8).[8]

8. The significance of the Minangkabao is evident in the following statement: "The
country of *Menangkabao* in Sumatra is, however, beyond dispute the parent country of
the Malay race. Menangkabao, contrary to all other Malay states, is an inland country"
(Crawfurd, 1820, vol. 2, 371, 372).

D. Sufi Influence Among the Malays

Another factor to consider in the spread of Islam in the islands is the Muslim mystical movement known as Sufism. Sufism has often been opposed by the legalists in Islam. Sufi extremism had led to its disrepute and neglect in modern Islam. Yet Sufism has supplied Islam's greatest missionaries to win converts in Africa, India, and Indonesia. It has also provided for a measure of spiritual care for the masses in traditional Muslim areas. Louis Massignon has remarked, "It is thanks to mysticism that Islam is an international and universal religion" (Williams, 1961: 136, 137; Ahmad, 1980: 135-38).

As previously mentioned, the spread of Islam to the Malayan race came after the defeat of the Muslim Abbasid empire state. Islam was spread by the Sufi mystics who came and lived their interpretation of Islam among the people without the support of any external authority. For example, they reinterpreted the Hindu drama, *Ramayana*, and filled it with Islamic content. A process of assimilation resulted in conversion to Islam of the Malay masses in Java and elsewhere in Southeast Asia (Gordon, n.d.: 3, 4).

> The second half of the 13th century saw a great upsurge of the *Sufi* evangelical movement throughout the world of Islam, and this was the main factor in the spread of Islam in Malaysia. (Fatimi, 1963: 23)

This does not contradict the fact that the Indian Muslim merchants helped in the spread of Islam. It is possible that these merchants were Sufis or greatly influenced by the Sufis. Some scholars have also held that Bengal is the main source of Sumatran Islam. This does not mean that the spread of Islam in the islands was due exclusively to Indian Muslims. Further evidence shows that contributions to the propagation of Islam in Southeast Asia also came from Arabian and Chinese Muslims (Fatimi, 1963: 25, 36).

Al-attas says of the influence of Sufism in Malaysia:

> I am inclined to believe that it was the *Sufis* who actually propagated and finally made it possible for Islam to become established among the people. With regard to Malaya, I feel almost certain that Islam was propagated by the *Sufis*. There may not be direct evidence to support this theory, but it is valid to the extent that there is circumstantial evidence in its support. (al-Attas, 1963: 21)

E. Islam Reaches the Philippines

The Sulu Archipelago between Indonesia and the Philippines served as stepping stones by which Islam entered the southern islands of the Philippines from Borneo and the Celebes. Thus the Muslim merchant and missionary brought Islam by way of India, Malaya, and Indonesia to the oriental terminus at the Pacific Ocean in the Philippines. With this the Muslim world extended from the Atlantic Ocean in North Africa to the Pacific Ocean in the islands of Southeast Asia, it is significant that in its initial spread Islam did not cross these two major bodies of water (Mathews, 1944: 87).

The earliest date of the Philippines and Borneo coming to the attention of the Chinese rulers is in the year 977 A.D. A trader by the name of Abu Ali is listed as having brought goods to Canton from Mindoro. Evidently, this was the same Muslim trader whose name appears again in the Chinese records in the year 982. This trade between the Chinese and the Philippines and Borneo continued over the following centuries (Beyer and De Vera, 1947: 29-31). According to H. Otley Beyer, a recognized Philippine anthropologist,

> the first specific date in Philippine history is 982 A.D., in which year an Arab ship arrived in Canton, China, with a cargo of goods from "Na-i," which is taken to mean the island of Mindoro. ("Mindanao Papers," 1955: I, iii)

He also states that "the Mohammedan empire of Malacca and its successors had an active part to play in the cultural history of Sulu" (I, iii).

Although much is uncertain about the exact manner in which Islam came into the southern Philippines, scholars would generally agree with the following statement:

> Whatever our doubts about the mechanism by which Islam came to the Philippines, its arrival from the south via Borneo is beyond dispute. Its rapid success there, more sweeping than in Borneo itself, is attested in Spanish history, and is still evident to this day. (Harrison, 1956: 44)

From Sumatra Islam spread to the other islands of the archipelago and entered the Philippines from Borneo by two different routes. One route was via Balabac and Palawan to Luzon and Manila Bay. The other route was via Tawi-Tawi and Sulu to Cotabato on the island of Mindanao. Islam is believed to have reached Sulu by the year 1380 (Lobinger, 1919: 62).

A legendary report of the early history of Sulu comes from a Filipino Muslim genealogy which states, "the first person who lived on the island of Sulu is Jamiyun Kulisa. His wife was Indra Suga. They were sent here by Alexander the Great." Another account tells about a later arrival in Sulu who became the ruler there in the person of Rajah Baginda. He is reported to have come from Minangkabao, Sumatra. (Muslim legend regards Minangkabao as the cradle of the Malay race and its princes are said to stem from Alexander the Great.) (Pickens, 1941: 5)[9]

The commonly accepted traditional version of the arrival of Islam in the Philippines declares that Islam was introduced in Sulu around 1380 A.D. by the preaching of a Muslim teacher called Makdum. This was ten years before the reported arrival of Rajah Baginda from Minangkabao. Islam was already established when Abu Bakr arrived in 1450 and married Parimisuli, the daughter of Rajah Baginda. One version states that Abu Bakr was also a descendant of Alexander the Great (whose name in Malay is rendered as Iskander Shah). This same Abu Bakr reportedly came from Mecca via Malacca, Palembang (Sumatra), and Borneo to Sulu. He was considered an authority on religion and law who propagated the doctrines of a Muslim preacher known as Abu Ishaq. After Abu Bakr married Parimisuli, he became the first to bear the title of Sultan Sharif[10] of Sulu. The sultanate established by Abu Bakr continues until present time in the Sulu area of the southern Philippines (Saleeby, 1963: 30-34; O'Shaughnessy, 1967: 62-63).

Cesar Majul, a Muslim historian at the University of the Philippines, suggests that Islam was introduced first by Arab or Persian traders in the Sulu archipelago in the fourteenth century and was later strengthened by contacts with parts of Islamized Malaysia. He believes that the sultanate

9. The early Indian Muslim teachers in Indonesia found it necessary to devise a substitute for the Hindu epics that had spread among the people. They developed the story of Alexander the Great as a champion of the faith of Abraham and a forerunner of Muhammad. The Malay royalty reportedly was descended from the marriage of Alexander to the daughter of Kaid, an Indian ruler (Winstedt, "Indian Influence in the Malay World," p. 191).

10. Sharif is a title for a descendant of Muhammad. In the Philippines it becomes "sarip" or "salip."

developed as an Islamic institution as a result of the gradual Islamization of the area.[11] He quotes a Roman Catholic priest, Francisco Gainza, whose description of the Islamization of the Maguindanaos of southern Mindanao is representative of what also took place at Sulu.

> The social institutions of these people must have been very similar to those of the rest of the Philippine archipelago until some Arab missionaries arrived and preached Islam to them. These established themselves in the Rio Grande in Maguindanao where they were well received by docile people. Introducing some religious practices, they married local women, learned the native language, and adopted many customs of the country and adjusted themselves to the social order. In time they were able to acquire many slaves to increase their prestige until they were able to join the ranks of the datus. Working with more unity, skill and coordination than the natives, and having slaves like them, they progressively increased their power and formed a sort of confederation among themselves until they were able to establish a monarchy which they declared to be hereditary in a family and from which the native datus elected a sultan. (Majul, 1964[a]: 9; cf. Arnold, 1913: 365)

In 1775 Captain Thomas Forrest, a British naval officer, visited Mindanao and reported that Islam had been there 300 years and that the tomb of the first Arab teacher, a Sharif from Mecca, was still known. Just as tradition gives Abu Bakr the honor of being the first sultan of Sulu, so tradition in Mindanao also gives this honor to Sharif Kabongsoan. In 1475 Kabongsoan is reported to have come from Johore, on the Malay Peninsula, to Mindanao where he introduced Islam in a peaceful manner and married daughters of local chieftains. Kabongsoan later extended his rule by conquering the neighboring tribes and forming the first sultanate of Mindanao (Arnold, 1913: 399; cf. de la Costa, 1961: 297, 298).[12]

11. In the introduction of the latest edition Cesar Majul suggests the possibility that the first Muslim missionaries to Sulu may have come from South China (1973: xiii). Saleeby believes that the Makhdum, who arrived in Sulu in 1380, was a noted Arabian judge who had previously established Islam in Malacca around 1350 by converting Sultan Muhammad Shah. Makhdum died in Sulu and is buried on the island of Sibutu (pp. 42, 43). Makhdum in Arabic means "he who is served" and is sometimes used as a title for a Sufi teacher (cf. Al-Attas, pp. 31, 32).

12. The following account of how Kabongsoan came to Mindanao is told: "Sarip

Emerson B. Christie gives the following account of how the Mindanao pagans became Muslims:

> The great Moro wave of immigration into the southern Philippines is a myth. What really happened is that at about the same time that Sulu was converted, Mohammedan Malays and Sulus, together with a very few true Arabs, came to Mindanao and while fishing and trading preached the doctrine of Mohammed. It is likely that if not in the earliest days of this preaching, at least shortly afterwards, these few outsiders had fire-arms, which of course were unknown to the natives. The rude unlettered aborigines, the Manobos, the Tirurays, Subanun, etc., could not but feel the great superiority of the new culture and gradually accepted the new institutions. Those who were converted were organized by their teachers into a petty state with an organization which, if rude, was still much stronger and more coherent than the primitive Malayan anarchy around them, and so the new converts themselves became a powerful force for further religious and civil conquest. The Maguindanao Moros, in fact, together with the Ilanuns, do not differ to any appreciable extent from the neighboring pagans. (Beyer and Holleman, n.d.: 18, 19)

The Spanish historian Antonio de Morga gives additional information about the history of Islam in the Philippines and indicates how recently Islam had penetrated the Philippines before the Spanish arrival to establish a permanent colony in the year 1565. In the northern island of Luzon, and also in Mindoro, the Spanish were able to drive out the Muslims. The same thing could have happened in the southern islands, if the Spanish efforts had been concentrated there at that time, because all indications are that Islam was just beginning to gain a foothold in the south when the Spanish forces arrived. This account by de Morga also gives information about the time and method of the spread of Islam in the northern Philippines. The

---

Kabungsuwan . . . set out on a sea voyage with a large number of followers from Johore. . . . A very strong wind blew and scattered them in all directions so that they lost track of one another. As a result Sarip Kabungsuwan arrived at Maguindanao. The others scattered to Bulunai (Brunei), Kuran, Tampasuk, Sandakan, Palimbang, Bangjar, Sulug (Sulu), Tubuk and Malabang (Maranao area)." The account describes how Kabongsoan persuaded the local *datus* or chiefs to become Muslims. They performed the ceremonial ablutions in the river where Kabongsoan had landed. As a result this spot was called Paigoan, meaning bathing place, and still retains this name today (Costa, 1961: 196, 197).

Gazizes and *Morabitos* mentioned in this Spanish account could refer to the warriors of the faith and the Sufi teachers, respectively. If the reference to the Red Sea is accurate, it could mean Arabian teachers from Mecca, showing a direct Arabian influence over Philippine Islam.

> A few years before the Spanish subdued the island of Luzon, certain natives of the island of Borneo began to go thither to trade, especially to the settlement of Manila and Tondo; and the inhabitants of the one island intermarried with those of the other. These Borneans are Mahometans, and were already introducing their religion among the natives of Luzon and were giving the instructions, ceremonies, and the form of observing their religion by means of certain *Gazizes* whom they brought with them. Already a considerable number, and those the chiefest men, were commencing, although by piecemeal, to become Moros, and were being circumcised and taking the names of Moros, had the Spaniard's coming been delayed longer that religion would have spread throughout the island, and even through the others, and it would have been difficult to extirpate it. The mercy of God checked it in time, for because of being in so early stages, it was uprooted from the islands, and they were freed from it; that is, in all that the Spaniards have pacified. . . . That religion has spread and extended very widely to the other islands outside of this government, so that now almost all of their natives are Mahometan Moros and are ruled and instructed by their *Gazizes* and other *Morabitos;* these often come to preach and to teach them by way of the trade of Ma(la)ca [sic] and the Red Sea, through which they navigate to reach these islands. (Blair and Robertson, 1909: XVI, 134, 135)

Pigafetta, the historian who accompanied Magellan on his voyage to the Philippines in 1521, makes reference to a Muslim called a "Moro merchant" in the account of the Cebu occupation. This Muslim was evidently a visitor and not an inhabitant of the Philippines; however, the King of Cebu had asked for his advice when Magellan requested permission to land. This Muslim merchant considered the Spanish to be no different from the Portuguese with whom he had previously come in contact in Malacca and also in the Muslim court in India.

After Magellan had been killed by Lapu-Lapu at Mactan Island, just off Cebu, the ship which Pigafetta was on continued on a visit to Tidor in the Celebes. Here they found Muslims who had been there for fifty years. Islam had been in neighboring Ternate for more than eighty years (Blair and Robertson, 1909: XXXIII, 18; Arnold, 1913: 388).

Francisco de Sande, the Spanish governor of the Philippines, in 1578 sent a report to King Philip II of Spain that indicates the widespread contact the people of Southeast Asia had with each other in Borneo. He states that in Borneo he found people from China, Cochin, Cambodia, Siam, Malaya, Java, Sumatra, Minangkabao, Acheh, the Batak area, the Moluccas, Mindanao, and other islands. This suggests the possible Muslim influence on the southern Philippines by virtue of trading contacts with merchants from these other parts of Southeast Asia (Blair and Robertson, 1909: IV, 131).

On June 27, 1588, the first Bishop of Manila, Domingo Salazar, wrote to King Philip II about the arrival of Islam in the southern islands of the Philippines, especially the island of Mindanao:[13]

> The law of Mahoma [sic] has been publicly proclaimed for somewhat more than three years by preachers from Burney [Borneo] and Terrenate who have come there — some of them even, it is believed, having come from Mecca. They have erected and are now building mosques, and the boys are being circumcised, and there is a school where they are taught the Alcoran. (Blair and Robertson, 1909: VII, 69)

Some anthropologists hold that Islam arrived in the southern Philippines at the end of the fourteenth century, but they differ on the manner it was introduced. This was a peaceful invasion by Arabian merchants and teachers who intermarried with the families of local rulers. They introduced Islam and were followed by Muslim missionaries. The spread of Is-

---

13. In the same letter the bishop makes reference to a Spanish ship falling into the hands of "the Lutherans" (pp. 66, 67) and regrets that "the Lutherans" remained free to attack and capture Spanish ships in Philippine waters with impunity. In all probability, he was referring to the Dutch. He also states that the natives of the Philippines have little regard for the things of God and the Christian religion, "seeing that we who profess to be Christians" pay so little attention to the practice of the faith. He adds, "Even the Moslems, at least those in the Philippines, did not compel anyone to accept their religion by force. They used persuasion and the example of a good life; that was why they had so many converts; would that the Spaniards who prided themselves on being good Christians would do the same!" (Costa, 1961: 104)

lam continued in Sulu and Western Mindanao among the pagan tribes. Gradually certain local rulers extended their influence over Sulu and western Mindanao as sultans. After becoming firmly established in this area of the Philippines, Islam was spreading into the northern islands when it came into conflict with the Spanish in the latter half of the sixteenth century. This was the beginning of a "holy war" that lasted for over three centuries (Cole, 1945: 194-98).

F. Summary of the Penetration of Islam into Southeast Asia

Many scholars point to the fifteenth century as the period when Islam made its greatest advances and became firmly established as one of the dominant religious forces in Southeast Asia. Islam came from Arabia and India into Sumatra in the twelfth century, to Java in the fifteenth, Borneo in the sixteenth. From these bases Islam spread to the Celebes and the Philippines (North, 1952: 99, 100). During the fifteenth century when Islam was threatening to engulf Europe, it was rapidly expanding in Asia and especially Southeast Asia. The coming of Islam to the Malays was due to many forces of history, culture, and religion. "The history of the spread of Islam in Indonesia can be written as the history of one protracted acculturation process the end of which is not in sight" (Nieuwenhuijze, 1958: 29).

It took a long period of time for Islam to become the dominant religion of Southeast Asia. It came in a peaceful manner. From the fourteenth to the nineteenth centuries, there was no organized Muslim mission effort in the archipelago. It was almost a spontaneous religious movement. Some sociologists believe that one of the main attractions to Islam was the opportunity to be liberated from the Hindu caste system. This was especially true for the lower classes. In Java this explains why the royal courts remained the last strongholds of Hinduism. The Muslim tenet of equality of all Muslims was a dynamic force directed against the Hindu social structure (Nieuwenhuijze, 1958: 35, 36; O'Shaughnessy, 1967: 66, 67).

The type of Islam brought to Indonesia by Muslim merchants was spread through long residence resulting in intermarriage with the local population. The simplest rudiments of the faith were introduced in a way that did not contradict the eclectic, monistic character of the indigenous religious beliefs of the tropical island world of Southeast Asia. An early Muslim trader in Indonesia expressed his feeling as follows:

So long as we live we are in the power of the ancestors of those who live in this land. We must therefore serve the ancestors of our heathen relatives. But so long as we do not eat pork and are buried in Muslim fashion we will wind up in heaven with our Muslim ancestors with whom we feel at home. . . . So long as we let our children become Muslims they will take care of the veneration of our souls. . . . Ancestor worship is for this life; Islam is for the life to come. (Van der Kroef, 1960: 268)

Summarizing the coming of Islam to the islands: it was introduced by Arabian, Indian, and Chinese merchants and mystics. It was welcomed by the people since it was simple and considered superior to their animistic, Hindu-Buddhist belief. The missionary of Islam, whether spice merchant or Sufi, was not a paid professional, but one who out of a sincere conviction that his religion was to be shared with all, taught what he knew of Islam by word and deed. The social aspect of intermarriage was also a contributing factor to the adoption of Islam as a natural outgrowth of such marital relationships. This removed the obstacle of approaching the people from a superior cultural and religious background, which has often been a problem for the Christian mission. The ease with which simple people could learn the basic tenets of Islam and the concept of allowing these tenets merely to supplement, not supplant, their previous beliefs also explain why Islam spread so readily and easily in Southeast Asia. By the ninth century Muslims had come to the islands, but Islam was not established among the Malayan people until the thirteenth century when Sufis appeared and presented Islam in an acceptable manner (Fatimi, 1963: 99, 100).

By the end of the fifteenth century Islam had come to the island world of Southeast Asia, and it had come to stay. In some areas of the islands it had not reached the interior or was not accepted in all parts with equal fervor. It could have been stopped from spreading further in areas that came under European hegemony as it was by the arrival of the Spanish in the Philippines. However, in the other parts of the island world of Southeast Asia, Islam was actually motivated and aided in its spread and penetration by the arrival of Western Christian powers from Europe. Thus the paradox, the spread of Islam in Southeast Asia attracted the attention of the Western Christian world to that area; the arrival of the Western powers in Southeast Asia resulted in the further spread and stronger hold of Islam in Malaya and the Indonesian Archipelago (Majul, 1964[b]: 335-98; Schrieke, 1955: 12).

3 A History of Relations Between Islam and the Western Church in Malay Southeast Asia

A. Contacts Between Islam and the Western Church

From the time of Islam's inception on the Arabian Peninsula under the leadership of Muhammad, Islam and Christianity have come into conflict. Although this conflict began on a small scale before the death of Muhammad in 632, in the century after his death it became widespread as Islam advanced into the Christian world of the Mediterranean Basin. As Islam continued to spread into Central Asia, Christianity suffered additional losses. Therefore, the more than thirteen centuries of contact between Christianity and Islam have generally been marked by hostility, suspicion, and misunderstanding. During this entire period the Christian mission has rarely been presented to Muslims in a positive manner. Kenneth Scott Latourette declares:

> In the thousand years between 500 and 1500, moreover, in the rise and spread of Islam, Christianity experienced what until the triumph of Russian Communism in 1917 was its most serious territorial reverse. Islam, while deeply indebted to its older rival, won from it much of western and central Asia, most of northern Africa and part of the Iberian Peninsula. (1937-45: I, xviii)

The Muslim attitude toward Christianity was strongly influenced by the contact that Muhammad and the early Muslim leaders had with the

Christians in the middle of the seventh century. The situation has not generally improved over the centuries. The Muslims in the Middle East still look upon the Christians as inferior. The various Christian churches have been isolated into distinct communities in Muslim lands. They have had a history of quarreling with one another, and Christians have generally been on the defensive. The Crusades left bitter memories in the minds of the Muslims. In the nineteenth century, Christianity was distrusted by Muslims because it was associated with Western imperialism in the Middle East. In the recent past some European powers supported Christian missions in Muslim areas sometimes out of political motives (Latourette, 1937: VI, 6-9).

B. Western European Christians Arrive in Malay Southeast Asia

Before the arrival of European powers in the Indian Ocean, the Arab and Persian traders were involved in a three-way struggle to gain control of the spice trade from the Indian merchants. One result of this was the spread of Islam to Southeast Asia through these Muslim merchants. Another result was to bring Muslim traders into direct conflict with Christian traders when the European powers began to penetrate this area in the beginning of the sixteenth century. The Arab traders brought an anti-Christian prejudice with them to Southeast Asia, and this was further strengthened among the Malays by the intrusion of the European Christian powers.

One of the earliest records of Christianity in Southeast Asia is from the year 1294. At that time a Franciscan friar named John of Monte Corvino traveled by sea through this area to reach the courts of China in the hope of converting Kublai Khan. This was the beginning of fifty years of Christian missionary efforts directed toward the Mongol court. As these missionaries traveled to China, they stopped in various Southeast Asian ports. They sent reports back to Europe, but no mention was made of any plans to evangelize the people there. Italian merchants brought back almost unbelievable reports about cannibalism and head-hunting by the people of Southeast Asia (Hall, 1981: 188-91).

It is one of the ironies of history that the success of the forces of Islam in Europe was a factor in leading the Christian powers of Europe to seek new routes to Asia. With the fall of Constantinople to the Ottoman Muslims in 1453, the Portuguese and Spanish were compelled to seek new sea routes to the source of the spices that were in such demand in Europe. This quest for a route to the "Spice Islands" led Vasco de Gama around the southern tip of Africa; the same quest also led to the exploration of America and the first circumnavigation of the earth by the Spanish seeking a route to the East by sailing west. This search for the source of spices brought about the introduction of Portuguese and Spanish Roman Catholicism to the island world of Southeast Asia.

Other nations, notably the Protestant Dutch and English, also sought their share of the lucrative spice trade and were soon venturing into the Orient. Colonial empires arose in India, Burma, Malaya, Indonesia, and the Philippine Islands. Thus the search for spices changed the course of world history by bringing contact and conflict between the East and the West. It also served to bring both Roman Catholic and other western forms of Christianity to this part of the world. Latourette writes (1958-1962: V, 416):

> On the eve of the coming of the Europeans, Islam also made its way into the region and became the dominant faith in the Malay Peninsula, in Java, and in the southern portions of the northern extension of the East Indies which was conquered by Spain (i.e., the Philippines).

C. The Portuguese Arrive in Malay Southeast Asia

The fifteenth- and sixteenth-century Portuguese expansion into Asia was motivated by commercial, religious, and adventurous interests. "Religious zeal, nourished in the tradition of the Crusades and the remembrance of the bitter struggle with the Moors in the Iberian Peninsula, certainly continued to be an essential motivation." Thus expansion into Muslim areas of Asia seemed a God-pleasing action to the Portuguese. Indeed Albuquerque, the leading Portuguese colonizer of this period, considered it an opportunity to destroy Islam and remove its influence from the face of the earth. His ambitious plans included diverting the Nile River so that Muslim Egypt would become weak with no more trade going through it, the capture of Arabia and destruction of the holy city of Mecca, and the elimination of Muslim influence in India. In a sense this was a continuation of the crusade ideology. As a result, the Sultan of Egypt sent word to the pope threatening to destroy the holy places in Palestine and to wreak vengeance on all Christians unless Spain stopped forcing Muslims to become Christians and unless Portugal stopped its voyage to the Indies (Schrieke, 1955: 37-39).

European influence began in Asia in 1498 with the arrival of the Portuguese explorer, Vasco de Gama, in Calicut in southwest India. He was looking for "Christians and spices" in his history-making journey around the Cape of Good Hope. When the nations of Europe discovered that the Muslim traders controlled the spice trade, they decided to break this monopoly and at the same time renew the assault on Islam that had become stalemated in the Crusades. This gave a splendid opportunity for getting a measure of revenge on Islam. Thus began a new "Crusade of faith and commerce" with papal blessing. The Portuguese soon controlled the Indian Ocean and Goa on the Indian mainland (Karnow, 1964: 12).

The Portuguese had a fervent zeal to destroy Islam and planned to use their superior ships to accomplish the task. They had learned that they could outsail the Arab merchant ships which were built only for sailing under favorable monsoon winds. An English historian, D. G. E. Hall, writes of Portugal's policy:

> Happily it was possible to serve God and mammon at the same time, for by striking at Arab trade in the Indian Ocean, Portugal aimed a blow at the Ottoman Empire, which drew the major part of its revenues from the spice monopoly. (1955: 197)

The German historian Leopold von Ranke has written of Portuguese aims:

> The intentions of the Portuguese were concerned directly with the centre of the Arabian faith. They desired to avenge Jerusalem upon Mecca. Their victories were once again fought and won in the enthusiasm of Crusaders. The Spanish operations, on the other hand, being directed against heathen, and not against Mohammedans, renewed rather the idea of the Northern Crusades. A grant from the Pope, a proclamation that "the enemy must be converted to Christianity or utterly destroyed," was all the justification that was necessary. (1909: 17)

The state of Malacca had accepted Islam and had become its stronghold. Malacca exerted its influence on Borneo, Sulu, and the Moluccas.

The arrival of the European "infidels" incited the Muslim Malays to missionary efforts to convert the animistic Malay population to Islam. This reaction to Portuguese intrusion resulted in Muslim mission efforts in Johore, the Celebes, in Brunei on Borneo and as far away as the southern Philippines and Manila Bay (Cole, 1945: 25).[1]

Malacca had become the most important trading center in Southeast Asia. It was also the main center for the spread of Islam to the islands in the south. The Muslim merchants from Gujarat near Bombay played a part in Malacca's conversion to Islam. These merchants shipped many tombstones with Arabic inscriptions to Malacca with a blank space for placing the name of the deceased. The Portuguese used some of these stones to build their first fort there. The epigram "Java was converted in Malacca" refers to the fact that Islam was spread to Java from Malacca through the spice trade. During this period Islam spread rapidly on the coasts of Sumatra and Java. This dominance of Malacca was successfully challenged in the early sixteenth century by the Portuguese, who gained mastery of the Indian waters and were thus able to conquer Malacca in 1511. This marked the end of Muslim suzerainty in Southeast Asia. From this time on the European powers contended against each other in this area (Mahmud, 1960: 484; Hall, 1955: 197).[2] As a result the Muslims lost the spice trade and, for a

1. After the capture of Malacca on August 10, 1511, Albuquerque tried to extend Portuguese control over the spice trade. In so doing, the Portuguese were aware that they were dealing a severe blow to the Muslim merchants of Syria and Egypt who were under the Ottoman Sultanate. Thus they were taking revenue away from the Ottomans and thereby assisting the Christian powers in the Balkans and the Mediterranean in their conflicts with the Ottoman Muslim power.

Vlekke also states that due to the Portuguese control of Malacca, many Muslim merchants transferred their base of operations to Brunei on the north coast of Borneo. Thus Brunei became a trade center where merchants from China came in large numbers. The ruler of Borneo accepted Islam and became an enthusiastic missionary. He gained control of Sulu in the southern Philippines at the time of Magellan's arrival in the central islands in 1521. No doubt this aided the spread of Islam in Sulu. After the death of Magellan, one of Magellan's ships, the *Victoria*, visited Brunei and later sailed south through the Sulu Archipelago where the source of spices was discovered in the Moluccas, but the Spanish found the Portuguese there ahead of them. They made the Portuguese aware of the urgency of strengthening their control of the "spice islands." Thus, they had to battle against the rapidly expanding influence of Islam, on the one hand, and their fellow Iberian Christians on the other (Vlekke, 1943: 74-79).

2. Pickens describes an interesting historical sidelight concerning Ferdinand Magel-

time, Lisbon became the spice center of Europe (Karnow, 1964: 41-43; Soebantardjo, 1974: 441).

The Achehnese Muslims in northern Sumatra set up a rival spice trading center and also spread Islam throughout the Indonesian Archipelago and the Malay Peninsula. "The conversion of the Malayan masses to Islam is due largely to the work of these Achehnese zealots" (Ginsburg and Roberts, 1958: 27, 28). Although the Portuguese conquered northern Sumatra in 1521, Islam continued to spread in northern Java and reached the area of present-day Djakarta by 1527 (Morgan, 1953: 375). The Portuguese by their un-Christian methods permanently gave a negative image of Christianity to the Muslims of Southeast Asia. F. W. Wertheim has said, "One can sustain the paradox that the expansion of Islam in the Indonesian Archipelago was due to the Westerners" (Fatimi, 1963: 88, 89). Hall reports:

> The Portuguese have been described . . . as swarming into Asia in a spirit of open brigandage. Against the Muslim peoples their crusading zeal stimulated rather than restrained their cruel and capricious behavior. Even their own historians were ashamed at their crimes in the Moluccas where the natives were driven into resistance by the injustice of their trading methods. And although priests and monks multiplied in their dominions, they were ineffectual missionaries because of the misdeeds of traders and freebooters. (1981: 206)

D. Sailing West Across the Pacific Ocean, the Spanish Reach Malay Southeast Asia

The fact that the Philippines' population is less than 5 percent Muslim while neighboring Indonesia is 90 percent Muslim is due not only to geog-

---

lan. In 1508 Magellan was a member of a Portuguese expedition that failed in an attempt to capture Malacca. Magellan was also a member of the 1511 expedition which captured Malacca. He was rewarded with the rank of captain for his role in the victory and was then sent on a trip to obtain spices in the Moluccas, just southeast of the Philippines where he returned later under Spanish auspices in 1521. He successfully rounded South America, crossed the Pacific, and claimed the Philippines for the Spanish crown. He met his death at the hands of a native datu, Lapu-Lapu, on Mactan Island just off Cebu. One of the ships finally returned to Spain under the command of Sebastian Elcano and became the first ship to circumnavigate the earth (1941: 12).

raphy, but also in large part to the policies of the Spanish in the Philippines. After Spain had lived under varying degrees of Muslim control for seven centuries, Spanish arms drove the last of the Muslim forces out of the Iberian Peninsula in 1492 following the battle of Granada. Spaniards arrived in the Philippines to establish a permanent colony in 1565. The Muslims had begun spreading out to the central islands and Luzon, establishing a stronghold at Manila. Gregorio Zaide calls the battle at Manila between Legazpi's forces and Rajah Soliman in 1567 a "miniature crusade; it was a fight between the cross and the crescent for supremacy. The triumph of the Spaniards over Soliman's warriors meant the victory of Christianity over Islam" (Zaide, 1949: 141-43).

Spain gave the Muslims in the Philippines the name of "Moros" (Forbes, 1928: II, 3)[3] due to the similarity of their religion to that of the Muslim Moors of North Africa. Although Spain was not able to drive the Muslims out of the southern Philippines, she did drive them out of Luzon and the central islands. The Spanish arrived in time to halt the Muslim expansion; therefore, Spain was responsible for stopping the Muslims in Asia. In dealing with the Muslims, Spain did not follow the peaceful policy that it applied in the other parts of the Philippines. The Spanish policy for the Moros was to conquer first and convert afterwards. The first of many attempts to conquer the Muslims in Mindanao and Sulu was made in 1578. There were some temporary victories, but Spain's efforts to subdue the Muslims in Sulu and Mindanao were unsuccessful for the entire three and one-half centuries of Spanish rule (Blair and Robertson, 1909: XXIII, 199).

In the early days of Spanish colonization of the Philippines the battle lines were drawn between the Muslims and Christians in Southeast Asia. This was looked upon by the Spanish as a continuation of the "holy war" they had fought against the Muslims in their homeland for over seven centuries. In this way the stage was set for the Spanish-Muslim Wars in the Philippines which continued intermittently from 1578 until the end of the Spanish period in 1898.

3. The word "Moro," from the Latin *Maurus*, was used by the Spanish originally to designate the natives of Mauritania in northwestern Africa and later the Moors and Muslims generally. By American usage the word meant any Muslim Filipino of the southern islands regardless of the tribal group to which he belonged. While "Moro" was once considered to be a derogatory term by both Muslim and Christian Filipinos, today it is considered a badge of honor, especially by young Muslims who wish to establish an independent Muslim nation called Bangsa Moro in the southern Philippines.

The Spanish Christian contact with the Muslims in the Philippines was more favorable to Christianity than that of the Portuguese in other parts of Southeast Asia. Yet the general result of the Spanish policy generated a hostile attitude toward Christianity on the part of Filipino Muslims. It also resulted in Filipino Christian attitudes of fear, suspicion, and hatred toward the Filipino Muslim. A Christian Filipino historian, Teodoro Agoncillo, has described the Christian-Muslim relationship in the Philippines as follows:

> One wonders why the Muslim brother has not been integrated into the Philippine body politic. There are obvious reasons. One is that as a non-Christian who has for centuries struggled for his individual identity he has come to suspect his Christian brother of betrayal, for the latter was used by the conquerors in the attempt to obliterate Muslim culture and religion. Consequently, the Muslim casts suspicious eyes on his Christian brother who, he thinks, is afflicted with Messianic delusions. There is nothing more abominable to the Muslim than to be told to discard his "Moro" way of life. Then, too, the various governments of the Philippines from the Spanish down to the recent times, have utterly neglected the Muslims, let alone the other minorities. Because of his fierce love of his culture and religion, the Muslim is looked down upon as an aberration — "a Moro" — with all its ugly implications. The result is that he becomes antagonistic to any attempt to bring him to the Christian society's fold, for he believes that this attempt is not made because he is loved, but because his conversion to the Christian way of life is necessary. The proud Muslim does not accept such imposition. (1960: 17)

To the Filipino Muslim, Spain was the aggressor who tried to drive him from his homeland. When the Muslims in the southern Philippines learned that Spain defeated the Muslims and converted the pagans in the northern Philippines, it is no wonder that they were determined to fight and defend their home and their religion to the last drop of blood. The frequent changes of Spanish governors with their differing policies toward the Muslims and the lack of intention or the failure to keep the treaties which the Spanish made with the Muslims led to centuries of bloodshed and the intensification of "the Moro problem." The after effects of Spanish policy are still felt today in Muslim-Christian relationships in the Republic of the Philippines.

E. The Protestant Dutch Replace the Roman Catholic Portuguese in the East Indies

By the end of the sixteenth century both the Dutch and the British had found the route to the Indies via the Cape of Good Hope. Thus they challenged the Portuguese for control of the spice trade. The Dutch found this to be a very profitable business, and in 1598 sent out five major expeditions that visited the ports of Java, the Moluccas, Sumatra, Borneo, Siam, Manila, Canton, and Japan. From the Netherlands some of their ships sailed east via Africa and others west via the Straits of Magellan around South America.

In 1600 the Dutch negotiated their first important treaty with the chief of Ambonia in the southeastern end of the Indonesian archipelago. They reached agreement to buy all the cloves produced there. The Portuguese tried to drive them out of the islands, but they were unsuccessful. In order to consolidate their various commercial activities, the Dutch formed the United East India Company on the pattern of the English East India Company (Soebantardjo, 1974: 441).

Spain attempted to assist Portugal against the Dutch in Southeast Asia to keep them from gaining a foothold in the islands, but by 1609 the Dutch controlled a large share of the spice trade and signed the "Twelve Years Truce" with Spain. The Dutch then endeavored to remove all competition and gain a virtual monopoly over the spice trade. This meant they also had to contend with the English, who had followed the Dutch into the area (Hall, 1981: 225-35).

During the Dutch efforts to replace the Portuguese, the Dutch enlisted the assistance of the Achehnese Muslims of Sumatra to fight against the Portuguese stronghold of Malacca. Later the Dutch persuaded the Sultan of Johore on the tip of Malaya to join them in driving out the Portuguese. In 1640 the fort at Malacca was captured by the Dutch. At this time many of the Muslim traders of Johore fled to Borneo, the Celebes, and the Moluccas in the eastern end of the Indonesian archipelago. The Achehnese lost much of their importance as Dutch influence made Johore a political and commercial power (Ginsburg and Roberts, 1958: 30-32).

It was to trade in spices and not to do missionary work that the Dutch had been attracted to Malay Southeast Asia. They established headquarters at Batavia (now Djakarta) in Java. In 1641, after the Dutch had driven the Portuguese out of Johore, they were able to dominate all trade with the Indies by applying savage military force against both the English and the Portuguese.

For 150 years the Dutch ruled the local chieftains in Indonesia with a strong, cruel hand. They forced the people to pay tribute and to supply spices on Dutch terms. This generated such hatred toward the Dutch traders of the United East India Company that the Dutch government was forced to take control of the situation by 1798. Some of the worst abuses were corrected. After the French invasion of the Netherlands, the English took over the islands of Indonesia from the Dutch, but reluctantly returned them to Dutch control in accordance with the Treaty of Amiens in 1802.

The Dutch government either discouraged or prevented all Christian mission efforts among the Muslims. It stopped the pagan practices of human sacrifice and mutilation and, at a later date, even encouraged Christian missions in pagan areas such as the Batak area in central Sumatra. In this way the Dutch actually aided the spread of Islam in Southeast Asia. The policy of religious neutrality, the government's fear of stirring up religious strife among the Muslims, and the initial prohibition of Christian missions in many areas, actually gave Islam a favored position in the eyes of the non-Muslim inhabitants of the Indonesian archipelago during the early decades of Dutch rule (Rauws, 1911: 242, 243).[4] After the Dutch opened up the interior area of Borneo, Islam penetrated there beyond the coastal cities and river areas. Before that time the jungle had acted as an effective barrier to the penetration of Islam (Scott, 1913: 319). Through the unification of the Indonesian archipelago under the Dutch, Islam was able to expand throughout the islands. Sufism's influence gradually faded out while more orthodox Muslim teaching took its place (Hall, 1981: 266-80). Thus the Dutch, as well as the Portuguese, contributed to the spread of Islam in the islands.

The policies of the Dutch continued to provoke local uprisings by their abuse of the leaders and the people. This involved the Dutch in costly military operations that greatly decreased their profits from the spice

---

4. These opinions of Dutch policy are made by Dutch scholars. Bishop Stephen Neill, a British missiologist, writes of the Dutch period in Indonesia, "throughout the whole of this period Islam continued to spread; in view of later history, it may be thought likely that if the Dutch had taken their Christian responsibilities seriously, whole regions could have been Christianized before Islam ever reached them" (Neill, 1966: 179).

trade. In controlling the spice trade, they followed the policy of "buy cheap, sell dear." In doing this they felt it necessary to cut down clove trees and other spice-producing plants where there was a temporary overproduction. This destructive, selfish policy resulted in reducing the natives in some islands to an unprecedented state of poverty and actually drove some of them into piracy. The natives were treated almost like slaves by their Dutch masters and were cruelly exploited for financial gain. In this manner the Dutch continued to expand their control from the Achehnese pepper trade in the north to the other spices of the Celebes islands in the south (Hall, 1981: 260-65).

In the last part of the nineteenth century there was another uprising among the fervent Achehnese Muslims in northern Sumatra. The Achehnese religious leaders proclaimed a holy war against the Dutch "infidel" that proved long and costly to the Dutch government. It took until 1908 to bring about effective control of this area. In the pacification of the Achehnese, the Dutch established good relations with Mecca and encouraged the Achehnese to go on the pilgrimage, the *hajj*, to Mecca. More liberal policies in other parts of the islands were introduced. During the first part of the twentieth century the Dutch finally began to realize substantial profits from the islands of the East Indies.

F. The British Gain Control of the Malay Peninsula

It has already been necessary to refer to the English due to their relationship with the Dutch. At one time the Portuguese and Spanish Roman Catholic powers combined to attempt to keep the Dutch out of Southeast Asia. Later the Dutch and the English joined hands against the Portuguese in attempting to gain a foothold in the area. After this, the Dutch and English fought each other for control of the spice trade. The Dutch gained the upper hand and dominated the area, with the exception of the Spanish Philippines, until 1824 when the Malayan Peninsula came under English control (Mahmud, 1960: 484).

In the interest of economic and military bases in Southeast Asia, the English established themselves in Penang, an offshore island of the Malayan Peninsula, in 1786 and in Singapore in 1819. These strategic bases made possible the penetration of the entire peninsula. The English had tried and had been unsuccessful in establishing permanent bases earlier in the Indonesian archipelago, in the Moluccas, and in Sulu in the Philippines. However, they did gain control over the northern portion of the large island of Borneo (Hall, 1981: 421-33).

In the first part of the nineteenth century, after the British gained control over Singapore and other areas along the Malayan coastline, they were able to exert greater influence over the interior by their tactful approach to the various Muslim sultans. By the end of the nineteenth century, the British administration implemented the Pangkor Engagement in 1874. This became the model for every subsequent treaty with the Malay States. This included the agreement that a British official would serve as chief adviser to each sultan in all matters except Islam and Malay customs (Provenchal, 1982: 146). Britain agreed not to interfere with either native custom or religion (Yegar, 1979: 261, 262). Thus the British government would not permit Christian missionary work among the Muslim population of Malaya, but it did allow mission work among the Chinese and Indian population of the area (Cole, 1945: 45-49).

In 1895, Johore, which had refused to join the federation of Malay States, ratified its own constitution. It provided for a Council of Ministers who must all be Malay Muslims and a Council of State made up of citizens of Johore regardless of race or religion. The British permitted this policy to become effective. As the British control over the Malay States expanded, the British resident in each of the states was given authority in all "matters of administration other than those touching the Muhammadan religion." This policy was first put into effect under Resident-General Sir Frank Swettenham in July, 1896 (Hall, 1981: 482-88).

G. Conclusion

An examination of the period of political history of Southeast Asia from the sixteenth century until the twentieth century reveals how Christianity and Islam came in contact in the island world of Southeast Asia. It has not been possible to refer to the political history without making reference to the mission history because they are so closely interwoven. It would be easier to understand this period of contact from a Muslim viewpoint if no distinction were made between the political and mission history, because the Oriental in general and the Muslim in particular knows of no such distinction. To the Malay Muslim the coming of the European nations into

Southeast Asia meant the coming of Christianity to this part of the world. The Muslims found the Christian forces fighting against them, trying to take the produce of their land and reduce them to virtual slavery. The Muslims also saw the Christian forces fighting against each other and even forming alliances with Muslim rulers to fight against Christian enemies. As a result of the political and economic policies of the Western Christian powers, the Muslims have an antipathetic view of Western Christianity.

4 Traditions, Beliefs, and Practices of Malay Muslims

A. What Is Islam?

"Islam is one of the main determinants of Indonesian spiritual climate" (Morgan, 1953: 3-5). This raises the question, "What is Islam?" There is no simple answer to this or the related question, "What is a Muslim?" The material below attempts to provide an answer, especially in regard to the type of Islam that is found in Southeast Asia.

Briefly, Islam means "peaceful submission to the will of God." This definition is based on the Arabic triliteral root *slm*. Muslim, from this same Arabic root, means "one who is submitted to the will of God." The Qur'an states: "Lo! religion with God is Islam." Muslims believe Islam to be the only true religion and claim it was the faith of Adam, Noah, Abraham, and Jesus together with his disciples. The primary mission of all the messengers sent by God has been to teach belief in the one true God and to establish justice among men. According to Islam, the last and greatest of these messengers was Muhammad. The Muslim then believes "God's latest revelation is given in the Qur'an; therefore, it is necessary to know the Qur'an in order to follow the straight path of Islam." Some Christian scholars hold that no religion makes conversion easier for both peoples and individuals than does Islam. Islam comes to a primitive people as a higher religion of a higher civilization. Its only demand to become an adherent is to profess with intention and in Arabic, the *Shahadah*, the Muslim Creed, which states, "There is no deity but God, and Muhammad is the Messenger of God." This creed represents the central, basic teaching of Islam. It emphasizes the unity of God and the person of Muhammad as the messenger of God (Hurgronje, 1906: 227, 228, 313). It becomes difficult to discriminate between a good Muslim and a poor Muslim. Snouck Hurgronje, a leading Dutch scholar, challenges the widely held concept that the Muslims of Southeast Asia are poor Muslims because they are ignorant of the main teachings of their religion. "Being a Mohammedan," he writes, "does not depend upon a man's knowledge of Islam, but rather upon his wish to be called a Mohammedan."

In the development of early Islam, pagan concepts of various spirits called *jinns,* demons, and sacred places in Arabia were retained where they did not conflict with the teaching of the oneness of God. These and other pagan concepts were generally transformed to fit into the overall teaching of Islam and made to serve the purposes of God (Watt, 1956: 313). As Islam left its Arabian homeland and expanded into other civilizations and cultures, which already had their own laws and customs, accommodation was made where these conflicted with Muslim law. The local laws were modified in different ways in different Muslim areas. This helps to account for some of the variety of customs found in the Muslim world.

Another major factor is the popular opinion in which the Muslim masses hold Muhammad. The Muslims have elevated Muhammad to a position similar to that which Christ holds in the hearts of the Christians. On the birthday of Muhammad, he is praised and called "the light of all light; he is the loveliest of all men; like a rose in the garden, like a pearl in the shell; through him all blessings flow." In the Islam of the masses Muhammad has become the helper of the faithful in this life and the intercessor on the day of judgment. Popular belief professes that whoever dies with the name of Muhammad on his lips will be saved regardless of the life he has led in this world. Conversely, whoever dies without calling upon Muhammad will not enter paradise no matter how pure and holy his life has been (Bethmann, 1953: 41).

In seeking to understand Islam, Hurgronje writes:

> In order to arrive at the basis of the significance of Islam in the lives and thoughts of the natives, it is, of course, primarily necessary to take into account what this Islam is, and what are the demands that it makes in practice as well as in theory upon those who profess it. (1906: II, 271)

The following presents an analysis of Malay Islam in the islands on this basis. What is true of Islam in Indonesia or Malaysia also holds true of Islam in the Philippines. Islamic countries have two main patterns which are often in conflict, the hierarchic and lay cultures. This is due to the relation between Islamic doctrines and the local culture that became Islamized. The Islamic pattern is recognized as more advanced and assumes more authority. It is represented in writing and adopted for social prestige. The pre-Islamic pattern has a strong undercurrent that exerts a powerful influence even on the intelligentsia even though it may be "officially" denied or deprecated. People who hold these views may be labeled as superstitious. The social position of a person may depend upon which influence is greater in his life.

There may be some adjustment and accommodation between these two patterns or traditions where Islamic teachers recognize popular tradition as a religion of the ignorant or tolerate local practices that are heretical from the orthodox viewpoint. According to some, Muhammad set the precedent when he converted a heathen pilgrimage into the Muslim *hajj,* the pilgrimage to Mecca, which every Muslim is obligated to make at least once in a lifetime. In this way local culture is integrated and "sanctified" into Islamic culture (Redfield, 1956: 48, 49).

Thus, local Islam is understood through serious study and attention to Muslims living in various areas of the world. Hendrik Kraemer states:

> Generally speaking, missionaries study far too little, but what is even more remarkable is the fact that study is mainly seen in the sense of studying in books behind one's desk. Little thought, however, is given to study of Mohammedan people, who constantly surround us, of their conditions and opinions; missionaries usually content themselves with a number of remarks picked up in conversation. They read books by Europeans *about* Islam and discuss it on this basis. They do not, however, plunge *into* the living forms of Islam that surround them and that should be their concern. (1958: 132)

What then is Islam? It is impossible to give a complete answer in a few words. Islam is a religion that stresses submission to the one God. Muhammad assumes a position of prominence as the last and greatest of the messengers of God. Islam may be blended with all sorts of local pagan beliefs and philosophic concepts, but it remains Islam. Thus, Islam is found in its many varieties in many parts of the world.[1]

B. Indonesian Islam

Not only is Islam in Indonesia different from that found in the classical Islamic areas of the world, but within Indonesia itself and within Southeast Asia there are found many different types and degrees of Islamization. It is almost impossible to make any generalizations about Islam in Indonesia or about the specific type of Islam that may be prevalent there. Nevertheless, this is an attempt to give some of the general characteristics of Indonesian Islam which are also generally true of Islam found throughout Malay Southeast Asia. A recent study of Southeast Asia describes Indonesia with its 90 percent Muslim population as the largest Islamic land in the world. However, the burning faith of Muhammad is hardly recognizable in the islands. This is evident in the small, simple mosques and Islamic schools. There is little evidence of missionary fervor in Malay Southeast Asia Islam, which is influenced by oriental passivity and tolerance. Islam did not really penetrate Southeast Asia until the late thirteenth century, more than 600 years after its conception in the Middle East. In passing through Persia and India, it lost much of its vigor. Islam did not require strict obedience to its laws, and the stress on equality appealed to the poor classes. Islam absorbed Hinduism, Buddhism, animism, and local customs in a syncretistic manner to gain the adherence of Southeast Asians (Karnow, 1964: 106).

Some scholars say that Indonesian Islam is only a veneer over a heathen foundation. This is supported by the fact that Indonesian Muslims follow certain customs and practices that are alien or even opposed to orthodox Islam. However, others argue that it should be remembered that Islam is not just the Qur'an and tradition, but that there is freedom for common opinion and practice within Islam. Orthodox and strictly traditional Islam can be found in Indonesia as much as in other Muslim areas. Therefore, Indonesian Islam is truly a part of world Islam. When an Indonesian claims to be a Muslim, his word should be accepted (Nieuwenhuijze, 1958: 39, 40).

1. For a complete, sympathetic, accurate understanding of Islam and what it means to be a Muslim, read *Muslim Friends: Their Faith and Feelings, an Introduction to Islam* by Roland E. Miller, 1995.

Islam in Indonesia tends to stress its extensive rather than its intensive aspects. The average Indonesian has a superficial and usually defective knowledge of the doctrines and law of Islam — few can read Arabic. There is some reciting of the Qur'an from memory; this is the maximum religious education for many Indonesian Muslims. Fulfillment of religious duties is as good or as bad as that found in other parts of the Muslim world. Many evidences of pre-Islamic religious practices can be seen in everyday life (Nieuwenhuijze, 1958: 41).

Islam in Indonesia is of many types due to the different tribal customs in different parts of the archipelago. The prevailing type of Islam, however, combines a fierce loyalty to Islam with laxity in the observance of religious duties such as the five daily prayers, the *salat*. This is true even of the faithful Achehnese in northern Sumatra. The pilgrimage to Mecca is more highly regarded than it generally is in other Muslim areas of the world. Whole families will share in the expense of sending one member on the *hajj*. It is the common belief that such a trip gains the forgiveness of sins. The pilgrim usually returns to his home in Arabian dress to signify his increased religious consciousness and commitment. The Muslims of Indonesia also like to honor the dead by visiting the graves of the "holy" men and women. They also have a tendency toward the magical and mystical elements of Islam which are sometimes based on pre-Islamic belief combined with Sufi teachings (Rauws, 1935: 101-3).

Justus van der Kroef's analysis of Islam in Indonesia states:

Indonesia is a nominally Muslim country, but the extent to which Islam has been accepted among its inhabitants differs greatly from region to region. At some native court centers and in such sections as north Sumatra, where Islamic influence made itself felt centuries before the coming of the Dutch, Islamic orthodoxy has always been conspicuous. In other areas traditional, animistic, and pantheistic concepts are more prominent. (1960: 265)

Although Islam in Indonesia may be considered by many to be only a "veneer," this does not make it any less important in the lives of the Indonesian people and nation. Islam is a significant factor in the lives of the Malays of Southeast Asia and has acquired the valuable status of being accepted as part and parcel of the culture. The type of Islam can usually be improved and made more articulate as long as the people consider themselves Muslims. In Indonesia the various religious influences did not reach down deeply into the daily lives of the people; they succeeded only in changing the names of the supreme object of worship to Shiva under Hindu influence, to Buddha under Buddhist influence, and finally, to Allah under Muslim influence (Mathews, 1944: 36, 37).

Norton Ginsburg, an anthropologist, wrote:

> Although Islam was a new influence in opposition to the older Hindu and Buddhist influences, it should not be supposed that it was non-Indian, for the Islam which was adopted by the Malays was not that of Arabia and Persia so much as an Indian form which had taken on many of the mystical formulations of Indian religions. Nevertheless, it was a break from the complete Indian dominance of previous centuries. India lost its pre-eminence as a sort of mother country, and the many gods of Hinduism were replaced by the concept of a single god. The Arabic alphabet replaced the Indian scripts, and Arabic words entered the Malay languages, replacing in many cases former Sanskrit. In these and many other ways — in eating habits, in clothing, in ceremonials — did Islam replace the former Hindu and Buddhist influences. (1958: 25)

The importance of Islam in Indonesian culture and history is also seen from the following remarks of A. Johns, a historian:

> One of the unifying themes of the history of Indonesia is the spread and development of Islamic religious life. And Islam at that which came orchestrated with various Indian and Persian accretions, and which was to grow mixed, to a greater or lesser extent, with local practices, animist or Hindu. So that a historical study of Indonesian Islam thoroughly documented by texts, carefully related to the social and economic background, is one of the fields of research which can throw light on the thought and life of Indonesians themselves. (Hall, 1981: 37)

The most concentrated Muslim area in Indonesia is on the island of Java, which is the most heavily populated of all of the islands and includes about 80 percent of the total population. The percentage of Muslims in the outer islands of Indonesia is far less than in Java. The Javanese Muslims have the underlying Hindu-Javan culture. The most fervent Indonesian Muslims are the Achehnese and the Minangkabao tribes in northern and western Sumatra, respectively. These two groups, who account for only a small percentage of the Muslims of Indonesia, are also considered the most orthodox (Bosquet, 1940: 1-3).

Indian Islam had been strongly influenced by Persian Islam with its Shi'ite teachings. Indian Islam has in turn influenced Southeast Asian Islam, which still shows traces of Shi'ite influence despite the predominant Shafi'i school of Islam throughout Indonesia. This Shi'ite influence can be seen in the celebration of the Muharram festival observed in parts of Indonesia and in the respect that is paid to Ali, Hasan, and Husain (Wilkinson, 1906: 3).

Among the Muslims of Southeast Asia, the term Malay has come to be synonymous with that of Muslim. To a lesser extent, this is also true of the various Muslim tribes throughout Indonesia and the Philippines. The inhabitants consider the Malay language the Islamic language of Southeast Asia. Thus during the Dutch administration of the Netherland Indies when the government promoted the use of the Malay language, they were inadvertently promoting the spread of Islam throughout the islands. Before World War II Malay was usually written in Arabic characters. The national language of Indonesia is a modified form of the Malay language called *bahasa Indonesia,* and today is generally written in the Roman alphabet.

A distinction is generally drawn between the types of Islam found in the "inner islands" of Sumatra and Java and that of the "outer islands" of the eastern part of the Indonesian archipelago. These eastern islands include the Muslim areas of the southern Philippines. The differences are far outnumbered by the similarities with the type of Islam prevalent in Southeast Asia. From the early penetration of Islam into Sumatra, a stricter type of Islam was introduced among the Achehnese and Minangkabao (Delius, 1935: 145-55).

C. Javanese Islam

Java was the center of the Hindu empire in Indonesia. Java today is the center of the government of the Republic of Indonesia. In Java Islam shows very little Arabic influence but displays a strong Hindu character. The Hindu-Buddhist civilization of Java was broken up by the Muslim invasion of 1475, and most of the people are now Muslims. Javanese Islam displays many animistic and Hinduistic survivals. Islam in Java is thus a rather primitive and tolerant type throughout most of the rural areas. A Dutch missionary to Indonesia, J. C. Rauws, stated:

> The religion of Java is Mohammedanism but it differs greatly from that taught by the prophet, or even from that found in the Near East today. Carried by the Arabs to India, it was deeply modified by Indian beliefs before it was transferred to the Far East. The faithful offer prayers with faces turned toward Mecca. They take part in Friday services at the mosque; they fast from sunrise to sunset during Ramadan, the ninth month; they abstain from forbidden food such as pork and most fermented drinks. The elaborate Hindu and Buddhistic worship with idols, temples and the highly organized priesthood fell before the militant Mohammedans, but belief in the souls of the dead, demons, spirits of the mountains and trees was undisturbed. The power of incantations, magic and even of the old-time medium still persists alongside the declaration that "there is no other god but God and Mohammed is his prophet." (Cole, 1945: 242)

The Javanese display a broad tolerance or even an indifference toward religion. They often say that all religions are equally good, and that everyone will be saved by his own faith if he lives up to it. They believe that to show hatred to those who differ from them in religion is contrary to the nature of religion. Thus in most areas of Java there has been little open opposition to the preaching of the gospel. Where the gospel has been proclaimed in Javanese homes, it has frequently been met with a positive response. Occasionally, even the Javanese Muslim leaders express themselves as favorably disposed toward Christianity. The Javanese Muslims are reportedly the most lax in the world in regard to the performance of the five daily prayers. Women are given a much greater role than in other parts of the Islamic world. One carryover from Hinduism in Javanese Islam is the prestige of the teacher called "guru,"[2] who usually has a following of Muslim disciples who go around begging. These men use Hindu and pagan chants to chase demons from the sick. Other evidence of Hindu-animistic

---

2. The Hindu Sanskrit term for teacher, *guru*, is still used by Muslims in the Philippines although the Persian term, *usted* or *ustadz*, is also used, especially in Islamic schools.

belief is seen in the shrines of Muslim saints and the mystical, theosophical Islamic literature to be found in Java (Mathews, 1944: 34, 35).

From the beginning of Islam in Java it was propagated in a mystic form that had both orthodox and heretical, pantheistic elements. It was taught that "what is, is God, and what is not is God." Another teaching proclaims that God is "Most High who is neither preceded by not-being nor accompanied by not-being, nor even surrounded by not-being." One of the early Javanese Muslim saints, Seh Siti Djenar, claimed to be identical with God. But he was condemned by his fellow saints. This mystical influence has led some scholars to think that Islam came from Iran via India and Sumatra into Java. The day of the martyrdom of Husain is observed by many families in Java, showing a Shi'ite influence. This influence is also found in Acheh in northern Sumatra and among the Minangkabao in west central Sumatra, who also observe the martyrdom of Husain (Morgan, 1953: 374).

The Javanese Muslims make a distinction between "white people," those who live religiously, and "red people," those who do not live religiously. It is reported that the number of white people is increasing through religious instruction, Islamic political parties, and international contacts with other Muslims. In Indonesian Islam the *salat,* the five daily prayers, is given the most emphasis of the five "pillars of Islam." The Friday noon service held in the mosque is considered to be compulsory and is thus the most popular. Special services during the month of Ramadan, the period of fasting, are even better attended. The time for prayer at the mosque is usually announced by beating on a drum made of a large hollow tree trunk with a skin stretched over one end. In the observance of the *zakat,* the practice of alms, the main emphasis is on the obligation to give to the poor of the community at the end of the fast of Ramadan (Morgan, 1953: 384).

In central and east Java, the Muslim population is divided into two groups. The *santri* are considered to be devout Muslims who observe all the orthodox practices of Islam. The *abangan* are nominal Muslims who practice parts of the religion of their ancestors, including Hinduism and Buddhism. The santri live in the urban areas as merchants. Most of the abangan live in the rural areas as farmers, and they lead completely different lifestyles. The santri have been a minority of the population and are beginning to exert a larger influence through religious schools, *Pesantren.*

One source says that in 1987 the santri were only 30 percent of the

Muslims in Java and added "hence Indonesia cannot be classified as a Muslim country" (Das, 1987: 226). In Indonesian Islam, there are much greater differences of faith and practice than in Islam in Malaysia.

D. Malaysian Islam

The Malays of the Malayan Peninsula were originally an immigrant people who adopted Islam in the fifteenth century. When Buddhism and Hinduism had swept over Sumatra and Java before the coming of Islam to Southeast Asia, Malaya had remained primarily pagan. The belief in spirits and the magic are evident in the Islam that is found in Malaya today. Nevertheless, the Malays of the Peninsula cling to their Islamic faith fanatically and are rarely found as members of the Christian Church in Malaysia. Today, they have a high rate of literacy due to the government support of village schools. The Malays of Malaya retain a body of superstition and ritualistic practices which are not derived from Islam. This deep commitment to pre-Islamic ritual and spiritual values remains among Malaysian Muslims today. There is no doubt that the Malays of the Peninsula are definitely Muslims, but this must be qualified by the statement that Islamic practice in Malaya is far from that practiced by the Muslims of the Near East. The Islam of Malaya does not detract from the faithfulness of these Muslims, but merely accentuates the fact that Islam is a living religion in Malaya.

The average Muslim of Malaysia looks upon God as a great king or governor who is very powerful, but also very remote from the daily life of the common people. Such a god does not trouble himself about a villager's affairs. The life of the villager is more closely related to beliefs in spirits who are comparable to local police. They may be corrupt, and they may be prone to make mistakes, but they take a most absorbing, personal interest in the life of the individual. Therefore, the Malaysian Muslim avoids offending the spirits and seeks to propitiate them to gain their good favor by various means (Cole, 1945: 7, 8).

Sir George Maxwell, in his book *In Malay Forests,* gave the following description of the Malay religious outlook:

> The Malays of the Peninsula . . . are now without an exception followers of the Prophet — decidedly unorthodox in many ways, it is true, but unshakable in their adherence to what they consider to be the essentials

of their religion: recognizing the claim of the "Law of the Custom," the *Hukom Adat,* the traditions of many centuries of paganism and Hinduism on the one hand, and on the other hand the often conflicting claim of the "Law of the Prophet," the *Hukom Shara,* their more recently acquired code — and always ready to make a compromise between them. In certain parts of the Malay Peninsula the pre-Muhammadan customary laws of debts, land tenure, and inheritance have prevailed over the Muhammadan Code and have recently in some instances been perpetuated by judicial decisions and by statutes. It is often said that the Malay of the Peninsula is a bad Muhammadan because he has retained so much of the pre-Muhammadan beliefs. It would be truer to say that he is an imperfect Muhammadan. . . . If he is told that his omission to say the five daily prayers, for instance, will insure his eternal damnation, he will be greatly distressed to hear it, but he will probably contend that this is not law as he knows it and thence proceed to try to persuade his critic, as he has persuaded himself, that a man should not be judged by the law but by the law as he knows it. (Mohd. Rasli, n.d.: I, 2, 52)

In summary, the rural Muslim of the Malay Peninsula is devoted to the religion of Islam and strongly resists any effort to change. Even though the type of Islam that is practiced there may not be recognized as orthodox by Muslims from the Arab world, yet it is a most vital part of the life of the Malay of the Peninsula.

E. Bornean Islam

It was from the island of Borneo that Islam came into the Philippines. Therefore, the type of Islam found in Borneo has a more direct bearing on the type of Islam found in the Philippines. There are three identifiable influences that make Indonesian Islam a definite religion through the entire area, including Borneo and the Philippines.

1. The environment, which is geographically and economically similar for the coast people of many islands.
2. Survivals of early "Indonesian," pre-Muslim ideas and customs, so strongly held that the new faith to be successful must either absorb or tolerate them.

3. A generally prevalent mental attitude of primitive superstitiousness (Scott, 1913: 322).

Among the lower class of poorer Malays found in Borneo — the artisans, small merchants, and fishermen — there was little incentive for them to adopt foreign customs from the traders who came there. However, among the leaders and wealthy traders of Borneo, it was advantageous to them to adopt the customs of the visitors. Thus, there are two different types of Islam among the people of Borneo, those of the upper class and those of the lower class. The lower class had many non-Muslim concepts, while the rich rulers and merchants of Borneo lost many of their pre-Islamic ideas through their cosmopolitan contacts. This upper class is also of superior intelligence and has gained a better understanding of the meaning of Islam. The difference between these classes is still evident in the type of Islam found in Borneo today (Scott, 1913: 326, 327).

Islam was successful in gaining followers among the Malay people because it was suited to the Malays' temperament and manner of life. It was also adapted to fit the Malays' situation. The superiority of the Arab traders and sailors is given as another reason for the acceptance of Islam in Borneo.

> The confession of faith, undoubtedly in Borneo as in the Malay Peninsula and Acheh, was regarded less as a creed than as a declaration of fealty. The Holy War against the infidel was held to justify their slave-hunting raids on the Dyaks of the interior, as well as the piratical attacks on European vessels. The Hajj across the partially familiar seas became to this boat-building, sea-faring people immensely popular, giving the Hadjis not only prestige and honor on their return but opportunities for a wider area of trade. . . . A great portion of the ritual prayers is neglected as not fitting in well with their life. The laws of trade of the Koran are ignored. . . . Muhammadanism was embraced eagerly just insofar as it fitted in with the habits of their life which had grown from the environment. (Scott, 1913: 323, 324)

Not only did Islam change the life of the Malays, the life of the Malays also changed Islam as it came into the area. The Malays of Borneo are Muslims who retain many animistic superstitions and a belief in the power of the magic in dealing with the cosmic powers.

F. Philippine Islam

Philippine Islam is an extension of Indonesian Islam as explained by a Filipino historian:

> The Muslims of the Philippines are racially, culturally, and religiously from the same stock (as the Muslims of Indonesia). Close proximity of the two areas of Mindanao and Sulu contributes still more to the development of closer ties. The Muslims of the Philippines feel as if they belong to the community which extends to Indonesia and looks toward Indonesia for religious and cultural inspiration. (Zaidi, 1956: 159)

Therefore, most of the statements that have been made concerning Indonesian Islam relate directly to Philippine Islam. Nevertheless, because of past differences in history and political development, there are differences within Philippine Islam. There are many different types of Islam throughout the southern Philippines. Therefore, when a general statement is made about Islam in the Philippines, it must be kept in mind that there are many possible variations. There is a distinction between "folk Islam" and "high Islam" in the Philippines. There is a predominant Shafi'ite Sunni influence blended with a Sufi influence, yet most Filipino Muslims are not aware of these influences or the distinctions between Islamic and non-Islamic elements in Philippine Islam.[3] Also, it is generally recognized that Filipino Muslims are not orthodox, even though they may observe the ban against pork and alcoholic beverages and other external ordinances. As elsewhere throughout the Muslim world, scholars distinguish between the Islam found in the rural areas and that found in the more heavily populated centers. "Generally, the 'more-Islamized' group dwells in areas exposed to urban ways while their 'less-Islamized' brothers are exposed to 'mountain' or rural habits" (Saber, 1961: 13).

Most of the Muslims of the Philippines can be classified roughly into two main geographical distributions. One-third are the Sulu Muslims liv-

---

3. In 1955 three Filipino Muslim congressmen were appointed to a committee of the House of Representatives to study the "Moro Problem." In their report they stated that 80 percent of the Filipino Muslims were "ignorant of their religion." It was estimated that only 10 percent could read the Qur'an due to the low literacy rates in the native dialects and much lower literacy in Qur'anic Arabic.

ing in the Sulu archipelago stretching from Mindanao to Borneo. This group also includes those Muslims living on the western tip of Mindanao around Zamboanga City. The other two-thirds are the Mindanao Muslims living in west central Mindanao stretching from the north coast of Lanao to the southern shores of Cotabato Province. These two groups include more than 97 percent of all Muslim Filipinos.

The Filipino Muslim practice of polygamy is, reportedly, an oriental rather than a religious custom. In the past there have been examples of Filipino Muslim leaders with as many as sixty wives. The Sultan of Sulu had thirteen wives at one period while the Sultan of Mindanao had twelve. The size of the harem is controlled by financial considerations and political alliances. The wife is thought of as a bearer of children and a servant. Muslim women are not treated cruelly, but they are looked upon as inferior to men. This is in keeping with Islamic practice in other Muslim areas. It is still possible for a Muslim woman in the Philippines to rise to a position of respect and influence. The veil is not widely used by women in the Philippines. Unmarried women are carefully restricted, but married women have considerable freedom. Muslim women have been known to fight beside their men in battles against their enemies (Hurley, 1936: 240-43).

The Maranaos who live around scenic Lake Lanao believe that windstorms, earthquakes, and other natural calamities are manifestations of spirits of former powerful deceased sultans and datus. The seasonal waterspouts on the lake are called *apo,* a pan-Philippine term for father or respected elder. The waterspout phenomenon is believed to be caused by deceased ancestors drawing water from the lake "to take a bath." The size of the waterspout is an indication of the importance of the person and a clue to discovering his actual identity.[4]

Victor Hurley describes a type of baptism that is practiced among the Muslims of the Philippines.

A Moro baby is baptized at the end of the seventh day. The ceremony is the occasion for a great feast. A priest moistens the child's head and cuts a lock of hair as the name is repeated. The name of the infant is selected from one of the seven names chosen beforehand by the parents. These

---

4. The author has observed these beliefs in both educated and non-educated Maranaos.

names are inscribed on separate sheets of paper and a small child a year or two old selects one of the slips at random. (1936: 269)

A description of the pre-Spanish type of Islam found in the Sulu area follows:

The Sulu is a Malayan of prominent type, reared in his infancy by a Brahman priest and brought up to maturity under the care of a Mohammedan instructor. He rejected his idols as early as 1450 and had been for more than a century prior to the arrival of Legazpi at Cebu a faithful and devoted worshipper of "Allahu Ta'ala," the Almighty and only God, according to the teachings of the prophet Mohammed and the holy Qur'an. He had laws, an established government, organized state, an alphabet, and a system of education. By trade he was a planter and fisherman, and both land and sea yielded him plenty. He turned the timber of his rich forest into boats and utilized the currents of the sea and the movements of the wind. Navigation came naturally to him and he sailed to distant lands and traded his pearls for silks and spices. He had a wide range of experience, and his knowledge of the world was by no means restricted to one island or to one limited group of islands. (Saleeby, 1963: 149)

Perhaps the most primitive of the Muslims living in Sulu are the Badjaos, who are also called the "sea gypsies," and the Samal Laut. Some scholars doubt whether the Badjao can be classified as Muslims. The Muslims of Sulu consider him to be a *Kapil* or a *Kafir*. The Badjaos spend their entire lives on boats. They are found throughout the Malay archipelago and have no fixed habitation. The Samals are considered to be Badjaos who have settled on land. Some Muslims living in Jolo also consider the Samals to be pagans.

A report for the United States Army on the people of Tawi-Tawi, an island near Borneo, was made by Lt. Bruce Stephenson in the early days of the American Administration of the Philippines.

A "salip" (Sharif) is a person descended from the prophet Mohammed. It is customary to worship at the grave of a "salip." People generally go to such a grave when they are sick or afflicted with some troubles, spread canopies over the grave, place rice and other foods and sometimes money on the grave, and pray and ask intercession of the "salip" buried there. These *salips* whose graves are important as dating back to the early days are buried in Tawi-Tawi Island. (Beyer and Holleman, n.d.: 24)

The Maguindanaos (or Maguindanaons) who gave their name to the whole island of Mindanao are the least studied and known of all the various Philippine Muslim groups at the present time. They live on the shores of southern Cotabato province and along the Rio Grande River which is known as the Polangi River by the Muslims. This is an inhospitable, sparsely settled area that is not easily reached and is a difficult place to live. The climate is hot and oppressive and most of the area is a vast swampland. During a period of heavy rains almost the entire area becomes a big muddy lake. While there are a few exceptions, most of the Maguindanao Muslims have remained illiterate and uneducated, and they do not seem to be progressing at the present time. In the past they provided leaders for the Muslims of Mindanao. Under strong leaders they were able to resist the efforts of the Spanish to conquer their area. The Maguindanao language and that of the neighboring Maranaos in the north are mutually intelligible.[5]

Several scholars agree with the report that the early Muslim leaders of Sulu came from the Minangkabao area of west central Sumatra. There is further evidence of Minangkabao influence among the Maranaos.

Here we find a strong mixture of the Malay with the aboriginal races. The people have preserved more of the art and architecture of Sumatra

5. The Philippine census distinguishes between the Maranaos and the Ilanuns (Iranons). All indications are that these are one tribe with one language. The distinction, if any, lies in the fact that the people living near Lake Lanao are referred to as Maranaos, while those living south of the lake near Malabang on the shore of Ilana Bay, are called Ilanuns or Iranons. Cf. Beyer-Holleman, Paper No. 162, Account No. 25, p. 3. "The Ilanuns form another minor element numbering only a few hundreds. They are the tribe whose main seat is on the coast around Malabang and around Lake Lanao." Clifford A. Sather of the Peabody Museum at Harvard University in a letter of April 26, 1966, to Fred Eggan, Director of the Philippines Studies Program of the University of Chicago, reports that he found some 4,000 Ilanuns living in Sabah (North Borneo) who seemed to stem from a mixture of Maranaos and Maguindanaos. Sather's interview with an Ilanun schoolteacher in Sabah revealed "that the Lake Lanao region of Mindanao is regarded by his people as their original homeland." This opens up a vast area for fruitful study to consider a "two-way" movement of the peoples between Indonesia and the Philippines.

than any other Moro groups in the islands. Their dress, buildings, and mosques could well be from Managkabau. (Pickens, 1941: 9, 10)

While the Maguindanao and Taosug Muslim groups have theoretically had a hierarchical type of political structure, the Maranaos have been divided into many smaller groupings under various datus often in conflict with one another. In 1927 this fragmented character of the Maranaos was described by J. R. Hayden, Vice-Governor of the Philippines, as follows:

> More than 100,000 petty *datos* hereditary leaders swagger about . . . no one of them admitting the existence of any native superior. Each *dato* is jealous of the other and zealous in maintaining his own power and prestige. (Mednick, 1965: 18)

Among the Taosug an Islamic religious hierarchy parallels the political offices. The Maguindanaos seem to have a similar structure with the religious organization interwoven with, and subordinate to, the secular administration. This is not true of the Maranaos whose institutions show little, if any, Islamic influence (Mednick, 1965: 19).

The Maranao trace two lines in their ancestry — one pagan, one Muslim. The pagan source is traced from Radia Indrapatra, who is believed to have come to Lanao to avenge the death of his brother Solaiman. Radia Indrapatra reportedly married the daughter of the king of the water spirits and built a house on the lake at Masiu. Two children were born before Radia Indrapatra departed from Lanao. His children settled in the fabled city of Bumbaran and had many children. Bumbaran was finally destroyed by fire and earthquake because the people there refused to receive one of the early Muslim missionaries who had been sent out by Muhammad. The population was destroyed except for three brothers who were out on a hunting expedition at the time of the disaster. The three brothers divided the area around the lake among themselves and this comprises the three main areas, or *pongampongs,* which their descendants still inhabit — Bayabao, Onayan, and Masiu (McAmis, 1976: 17).

While these Bumbaran refugees are considered by the Maranao as the "original" inhabitants of the Lake Lanao area, the most important ancestor is the Muslim missionary, Sarip Kabongsoan. Most Maranao genealogies start with him, although some go back to Muhammad or all the way back to Adam and Eve. The Maranao folktale *(totol)* is that Sarip Ali migrated to

Johore and married the daughter of Iskander Diukarnine (Alexander the Great), the Sultan of Johore. Seven sons known as "the seven sarips" were born of this marriage, and they are credited with bringing Islam to the Philippines, Borneo, and the Celebes. One version of this story follows:

A sister of the Seven Sarips, Putri Tomania, disappeared in infancy. Mourning for their lost sister, the seven brothers set out in as many boats to seek her. A storm came up at sea and separated their vessels. One was blown to Brunei in Borneo, another to Sulu, a third to Menado (Celebes), a fourth to Makassar (Celebes), a fifth to Luzon. Two were blown to Mindanao; Sarip Ali who landed on the north coast near the present site of Cagayan de Oro (Misamis Oriental Province) and Sarip Kabongsoan. Sarip Kabongsoan was the oldest brother, and he landed at the mouth of the Polangi (Cotabato) River. This was the area in which many years earlier Putri Tomania had been found. Two brothers had been cutting bamboo for a fish corral and on cutting one down had heard a cry within it. Opening it up, they discovered an infant girl whom they took home and raised. She grew up to be a beautiful woman, and when Sarip Kabongsoan met her, he did not recognize his long-lost sister, and married her. The Sarip also contracted two additional marriages, one on the coast to the north of the river at Malabang, the other up the river from the coast. Each of these marriages was to the daughter/ sister of a local ruler. Because of his influential affines, his personal character, and excellence of the faith he brought, the people of Cotabato (i.e., the Maguindanao) converted to Islam. (Mednick, 1965: 96, 97)

While the Maranaos have received influence from Indonesia, Borneo, and Malaya, it has generally been indirect and less significant than in Maguindanao and Taosug areas. Most Maranao contacts with other Muslims have been via the Maguindanao. Malay documents and speakers of the Malay language have been found among the Maguindanao, and Spanish sources mention Maguindanao alliances with peoples in Borneo and Celebes. No reference to similar contacts is made for the Maranaos. Mednick's study also states:

Another index of Maranao isolations is to be found in their practice and knowledge of Islam. Kuder (1949) notes that among their co-religionists the Maranaos are considered to be backward. My own comparative impressions would confirm this. The number of persons having a direct knowledge of Islam in the sense of being able to read directly from the Koran appear to be fewer even in such Maranao centers as Marawi City than in comparable Maguindanao centers such as Cotabato City or Tao-sug centers such as Jolo. . . . Various pagan beliefs, particularly in regard to river spirits and propitiation of the dead, remain prominent in the Maranao system of religious belief. (Mednick, 1965: 31, 32)

All those who speak the Maranao language consider themselves to be a single structure of institutions, values, and beliefs. The phrase *pongampong a ranao,* encampment of the lake, means much more than the aggregation of a number of sociopolitical units; it includes the conscious awareness of sharing a single language and culture and being adherents of a universal religion, Islam. Therefore, to be a Maranao means to be a Muslim. According to Mednick, all Maranaos trace their Muslim ancestry back to Kabongsoan.

The framework of the society is genealogical and is evidenced by traditional, written genealogies called *salsilla.*

All legitimate members of Maranao society must, in theory at least, be able to find a place on a *salsilla,* and, thus, to indicate descent from the prime ancestor, Sarip Kabongsoan. (Mednick, 1965: 42, 43)

Despite the imperfections of Islam as it is found in Maranao society, Islam remains its most outstanding characteristic according to Mamitua Saber, a Maranao sociologist.

To the bonds created by the network of social relations are added those of a belief. A Maranao when asked to identify himself will most usually declare that he is a "Moslem" or a "Moro." . . . Although there are frequent departures from the strict interpretation of Koranic Law, the notion that Maranao customary law is, ultimately, divinely derived and sanctioned plays an important part in the settlement of conflicts and disputes which constantly threaten the unity of the society. (Saber, 1957: 45, 46)

Thus, the Maranao considers Islam the most significant characteristic in his way of life. The Maranao language is considered the Muslim dialect of the Lake Lanao area. Departures from orthodox Islam are considered to be permissible and sanctioned by *ijma,* community agreement.

The Maranaos believe that *kabarat,* supernatural power, is a gift of grace to certain individuals. A lesser supernatural power is known as *kabatua.* Such supernatural qualities are considered as actual physical substances translated from parents to certain special offspring. A man who has *kabarat* can be both a religious and political leader among the Maranaos (Saber, 1957: 67).[6]

The large freshwater lake around which the Maranao lives and from which he gets his name is a major religious symbol. The ablutions before religious worship and prayer are performed in the lake. The Maranao "believes his religion commands him to relieve himself and wash himself in the lake, and because this same water must then be used for drinking and cooking, sanitation and health are made problematic" (Bennett, 1964: 220).

A report that was made when General John J. Pershing was still active in the Lake Lanao area during the early days of the American administration of the Philippines can be reiterated today.

> They profess the Mohammedan religion but are generally ignorant of its requirements. The Koran is esteemed as their gospel but is rarely seen and found, so far as ascertained, in the hands of *panditas.* They are fatalists, declining even to boil water to prevent the cholera infection, saying that if God wishes them to die, they will die, and if not, they will not die. (Beyer and Holleman, n.d.: 3, 4)

Maratabat is thought to be unique among the Maranaos and to contain the key to Maranao "psychology." *Maratabat* is often defined as "face," "pride," or "Amor propre," but it is more than that among the Maranao. *Maratabat* helps explain the life and conduct of the Maranao in his daily life. A Maranao will go to great lengths to build a "good" *maratabat.* Hav-

---

6. The Maguindanaos share this belief. A Spanish account of 1691 describes how the Muslims believed that their leader, Sultan Kudrat, had supernatural powers. Reportedly, he could make fish leap into his boat, make cannons float, and predict coming events. The Maguindanaos obeyed him and considered him a saint. The Spanish feared that after his death the Maguindanaos would worship him and establish another Mecca in Mindanao (Blair and Robertson, 1909: 40, 138).

ing a bad community image is considered "having dirt on his face," and this will provoke a Maranao to go to any extreme to remove any "stain" from his *maratabat*. *Maratabat* is operative primarily within the Maranao social organization and is carried over from one generation to the next.

"*Maratabat* is an ideology." It is commonly used by the Maranaos to refer to "psychological substance." This ideal is reflected in the Maranao epic, *Darangan,* in which the hero is a model for Maranao *maratabat.* "*Maratabat* is an expression of one's social position." The higher the social rank of the Maranao, the greater is his *maratabat,* and also the greater the need to exhibit and defend his *maratabat.* "*Maratabat* is sustained by social coercion, not by individual choice." "*Maratabat* is legal in terms of traditional and customary law." This is impressed on the Maranao from childhood. Thus *maratabat* is in Maranao society a compelling social motive accepted by all who wish to remain respected members of that society (Saber and Tamano, 1961: 10-15).[7]

Except for the drum, which called a Muslim to prayer instead of the voice of the muezzin from the minaret, the Muslim prayer service among the Maranaos was fairly similar to that practiced throughout the Muslim world. It was outside the mosque that deviations from orthodox Islam were found. The *kalilang* was held as a feast of various spirits. A feast to the river spirit was held with small boats filled with food and placed on a raft to float down the river. The *paraian* is a bamboo pole that was placed in the center of the field with food offered to the spirits. Sometimes Arabic verses from the Qur'an were used instead of food. These were offered at times of planting and harvest.

The Sufi practice of worshiping and honoring the dead was not unknown among the Maranaos. A famous Maranao who was killed fighting the Spaniards was Sabir sa Radapan of Radapan, Lanao Norte, which is a few kilometers from Linamon. When pilgrims made visits to his grave, they gave offerings of food to the caretaker. The grave was covered with an umbrella which is the symbol of royalty throughout Southeast Asia.[8]

---

7. The Maranaos themselves explicitly recognize this relationship and state it in a number of common phrases: a man who has lost his *bangsa* (identification with ancestors) has no *maratabat;* a man without *maratabat* is nobody; or a man who loses his *maratabat* becomes very, very small; and an important man is one with lots of *maratabat.*

8. The Reverend David Hamm, a Congregationalist missionary who spent twelve years teaching at Dansalan Junior College in Marawi City, reports that he went along on

G. The Role of *Adat* in Malay Islam

Malay customs are a part of the Malayo-Polynesian culture, which extends from Madagascar to Formosa to New Zealand! These primitive foundations had been affected only slightly by various Muslim laws. In Java, rules for Muslim marriage and divorce are followed, but property allocation stems from Indonesian tradition. Generally speaking, Muslim law is subordinated to local tradition. In Indonesia even the wife can obtain a divorce, which under Shafi'i law is very difficult (Bosquet, 1940: 9, 10).

The process of the Islamization in Indonesia is still taking place today. In no part of Indonesia had the *Shari'a,* "Muslim law," completely replaced *adat,* local customary law. The laws of marriage, family relationship, and inheritance are largely governed by *adat* rather than the *Shari'a.* The Minangkabao tribe, which has been Muslim for centuries, still follows a matrilinear clan system (Prins, 1951: 285). Tradition, *adat,* is the all encompassing pattern of life for every member of the community. In important matters of life there is no choice while in minor areas of life there is much freedom. In *adat* normative myth and everyday life with its changes meet on a common ground. *Adat* thus becomes the standard by which to live. Indonesian culture has always been based on the closed community life where all is governed by the elders according to *adat* (Nieuwenhuijze, 1958: 10, 38, 39, 80; cf. Ter Haar, 1962).[9]

The Achehnese Muslims in northern Sumatra are strongly guided by *adat,* which has evolved over the centuries. The *adat* changes from generation to generation. The most important laws are those that are not set down in writing but are kept through proverbs or familiar sayings in the oral traditions. The Arabic laws have only a limited influence on the masses. The Achehnese believe that *adat* and *hukom,* which is the term for religious law, should take their place side by side in a good Muslim community. However, in practice the *adat* governs most of life while *hukom* influences only a small portion. The people see no conflict with Islam when

---

several visits to this grave by invitation of the Imam of Marinaut who had vowed to make a pilgrimage to Sabir's grave if the Imam's son recovered from an illness. Other Maranaos visited the grave to seek a cure for various sickness.

9. B. Ter Haar, *Adat Law in Indonesia,* edited and translated from the Dutch by E. Adamson Hoebel and A. Arthur Schiller (Djakarta: Bhratara, 1962). Originally written as a textbook for Indonesian law students. Identifies nineteen areas of the archipelago that have distinctive *adat.*

they follow *adat* even when it actually contradicts Islamic law.[10] As mentioned, *adat* can change from generation to generation despite the popular belief that it is "unchangeable law" or custom. In Malay culture "the most important laws are those which are not set down in writing." When laws must be put in writing, it is a sign that they are falling into disuse or decay. *Adat* controls the life of the people and can be determined only by living among the people and observing their daily life.

H. The Role of Sufism in Malay Islam

Sufism is the name given to the mystical practice in Islam (al-Attas, 1963). There is a wide difference of opinion on how much of an influence Sufism has played and presently plays in Islam in the islands. James Thayer Addison has called it "the outstanding characteristic of the Moslem Indies." He believed that this was due partly to the natural inclination of the people, partly to their heritage of Hindu teaching and practice, and partly to the type of Islam that has been propagated in Southeast Asia.

> Sufism, or mysticism, and particularly pantheistic mysticism, found fertile soil in Indonesian spiritual and emotional life from the very beginning because of the nature of the Indonesian mind and because of the age-old influence of Hinduism and Buddhism. Moreover, Islam was introduced in Indonesia by Indians. (Morgan, 1953: 395)

Sufi doctrines were taught in northern Sumatra in the sixteenth and seventeenth centuries. Some Sufi teachers exerted great influence. The founders and leaders of various Sufi orders are given divine honor and worship by their followers. The work of al-Ghazali (the foremost Islamic philosopher and mystic, d. 1111) has been known in Indonesian and Malay languages for over two centuries. His influence is widespread in Arabic schools. Al-Ghazali helped to return Sufism to orthodox Islamic teachings (Morgan, 1953: 395).

Some Sufi teachers in Sumatra taught that Muslim tradition and law were no longer necessary and that those who live in communion with God

---

10. An Achehnese proverb states, "*Hukom* and *adat* are inseparable, even as God's essence and His attributes."

are above ritual and law. They believe that complete communion with God rules out the distinction between the creature and the Creator. These Sufi teachers gained wide influence in the social and moral life of the people. Both orthodox and heretical Islamic mysticism have exerted a strong influence in Indonesia. Heretical, pantheistic mysticism has continued to exist even though orthodox Sufism became more widely known. Many politicians and intellectuals practice the disciplines of the inner life of mysticism (Morgan, 1953: 402).

Winstedt describes Indian influence on Indonesian Islam as follows:

> Like their early Indian teachers, Malay Muslims, although orthodox *Sunnis* of the *Shafe'te* school, formerly worshipped saints both living and dead, split themselves into sects and accepted a pantheism that was not as in Arabia the speculation of a few, but as in India the faith of the mosque and marketplace. The worship of saints countenanced the continuance of time-hallowed offerings at the graves of ancestor, ruler, and teacher. And the gods of the Hindu pantheon became genies, infidel it is true, but for a long while not vanished from invocation or from charms for the lover and the warrior. (Winstedt, 1944: 191)

The Malay Muslim frequently is seen at the grave of some famous Muslim Sufi saint. A Muslim vows to bring offerings to the saint if he will answer his petition. A piece of cloth is then tied to a nearby tree to remind the spirit of the saint of the petition. The Qur'an is also believed to have magical power when a verse is written on paper and swallowed by a sick person (Mathews, 1944: 164-67).

The early Sufi influence in Indonesia was later tempered by more orthodox forms of Islam as contact with Arabia and Egypt increased. Yet, even the orthodox teachers have found it expedient to use mysticism to maintain a hold on the masses. It has been said that "every Muslim teacher of any note tries to give instruction in mysticism, because only by so doing can he get any real hold on the people." The Sufi recitation of *dhikr*, meaning a remembrance, is popular throughout the Malay world. The influence of Sufism on Malay Islam is not immediately evident because it is not present in an institutional form. Nevertheless, Sufism continues to be a vital influence at all levels and in all types of Islam in the islands, even when the adherents are not aware of Sufism in their belief and practice.

I. The Role of Education Among Malay Muslims

Indonesian children are taught to recite the Qur'an by a *guru* or *usted,* both terms meaning teacher in Sanskrit and Persian, respectively. When a Muslim child has mastered the introductory studies of Islam and is proficient in reciting the Qur'an, a family feast called a *slametan* is held. The Muslim children learn about ritual purification and performance of the daily ritual prayers. They learn about expressing the proper intention to fast during Ramadan. There are also advanced schools for the study of Islam which are called *pesantren.* Some of these are quite large and offer courses in various branches of Islamic theology. In Sumatra a *pesantren* is called *madrasah.*

The religious leaders in the mosques and religious schools are held in respect because of pre-Muslim tradition. The masses held these teachers in awe because they could read the sacred books. The only ones who have more respect are the *Hadjis* who have been to Mecca. Sometimes these religious teachers, who are called the *ulema,* are the people who support the local political rulers, and sometimes they are in competition with them.

Clifford Geertz, an anthropologist who has spent much time doing field-work and research, especially in Java, declares that the Muslim schools are the main factor in establishing Islam firmly within Indonesia.

> The Moslem educational system is the master institution in the perpetuation of the Islamic tradition and the creation of an Islamic society, as well as the locus of the most serious efforts to modernize that tradition and society presently being pursued. . . . Without the *pesantren* and later the *madrasah* and *sekolah Islam,* Indonesia would not have become even a nominally Islamic society from the simple circumstances of contact. (Geertz, 1963: 10)

The role of the school was vital in establishing Islam in Indonesia, and the role of the Muslim school at present is also vital in bringing about a modernization of Islam in Indonesia.

> Today as in the past the school is the lifeline of the Islamic tradition and the reformed school is that tradition's path to the present. It is essential that this path should not be blocked by shallow and short-sighted "modernization" policies which attempt to catch up with the West by a mindless imitation of its external forms. (Geertz, 1963: 17)

The above gives some indication of the important role the school has played, and is presently playing, in establishing and modernizing Islam throughout Malay Southeast Asia. This is a subject worthy of much more consideration and study than can be given here.

J. Distinctive Beliefs and Practices Among Malay Muslims

In all areas of the Muslim world there is a distinction made between what is called "high Islam" and "folk Islam." The same holds true among Malays. It is sometimes a blending of the two that makes it virtually impossible to distinguish whether a certain belief or practice should be classified as high Islam or folk Islam or in some area between the two. The following beliefs and practices are generally considered to be those of folk Islam as it is found among Malays. In describing the religious beliefs of Southeast Asia, Basil Mathews, a British missiologist, says that the common substratum of the Buddhists, Muslims, Hindus, Confucianists, and some Christians is animism. This is especially influenced by the belief, common throughout the Orient, in the spirits of ancestors exercising control over present-day life (Mathews, 1944: 2; Bosquet, 1940: 59).[11]

The family group is important in Malay life where members of society are sometimes linked to deified ancestors who first gave the *adat*. Malay religious systems seem to be monistic, in that they stress close identity between the material and the spiritual. Thus, the concept of God tends to be all-inclusive. God is not thought of so much as a personal being separate from his creation, but rather as the aggregate of all supernatural forces, a godhead, which can be seen in many different ways. Van der Kroef describes the indigenous religious view of Southeast Asia as follows:

Basic to the cosmology of these indigenous religious systems is the monistic unity of all reality in which Godhead and man, the supernatural and natural order, continuously intertwine, and in which sharply delin-

11. A major factor in the demographic problem of Indonesia is due to the Javanese concept of ancestor worship. Family ties are so strong that birth control is virtually impossible. Already four-fifths of the total Indonesian population live on one-tenth of the land area on the island of Java, making Java the most densely populated area in the world.

eated and conceptualized distinctions between objects are blurred and paradox seems to illustrate higher unity. It cannot be emphasized enough how basic — and how essentially similar in different Indonesian cultural strata, from Sumatra to the Moluccas — this cosmology in its religious framework is to the entire traditional social process. (1960: 267)

In the Malay Muslim community the Christian concept of original or inherited sin is lacking, as it is in Islam in general. However, there is a concept of sin and individual responsibility in the Qur'an. At the close of the prayer, *salat,* the Muslim asks for forgiveness of sins. Transgression of the *adat* of the ancestors is called *dosa.* Christians in Malay Southeast Asia have adopted this word to convey the idea of sin. On the other hand, to break the Muslim laws or prohibitions in regard to food is known as *haram,* which has about the same meaning as the word "accursed." This would indicate that for the Muslims a breach of ritual is considered to be a greater offense than the breach of some moral transgression or *adat* (Simon, 1912: 173).

Kraemer's analysis of the Malay Muslim idea of sin states:

The indigenous idea of sin is imperfection, weakness. This imperfection, this weakness, is essentially innocent, for it is inherent in man's *kordat,* his nature. The notion of sin as guilt, man's ineffaceable guilt for which he is personally responsible, as a state of being irrevocably rejected before God, resulting in our having been cast out of the life and communion with God which is essentially necessary for being truly man, this notion is absent. I can only shortly indicate the underlying fundamental reason: the natural, naturalistic monism of primitive man, where the concept of God is actually completely absorbed into the concept of man. Since this notion of sin is lacking, the remission of sins is not a miracle, but self-evident. Surely man cannot be held guilty on account of his innate imperfection and weakness. Forgiveness is God's profession. That they, nevertheless, speak of God's merciful forgiveness is partly due to the influence of Islam, . . . but also derives from the general notion that, besides man who cannot help being imperfect, there is a sovereign and omnipotent God, who, being sovereign, may do as he pleases, of course. In the primitive mind, man and God have no *moral* relationship. (1958: 134)

Many Muslims have only a superficial knowledge of religious teaching. Most Malay Muslims believe that God readily forgives and is full of grace, mercy, and charity. The belief in angels, devils, and *jinns* gives opportunity for the pre-Islamic spirits to continue in popular belief. There is a belief that a good or evil spirit lives in every Muslim weapon. The average Malay Muslim believes in the Qur'an as the word of God, but he knows little of the actual content of the Qur'an.

The Malay Muslims have a deep reverence for Muhammad and usually hold a big celebration on the anniversary of his birth. Amulets made at this period have special powers when worn about the neck.

The dead are remembered on the third, seventh, fortieth, hundredth, and thousandth day as well as annually. "All Souls' Day" is observed sometimes with meals in commemoration of the dead.[12] Fate or belief that God determines human action for years to come on a certain night each year is a common belief. Uneducated Muslims believe that if they can recite the Arabic words of the Qur'an correctly, even without understanding the meaning, God will bless them and save their souls (Morgan, 1953: 391, 404).

In folk Islam many unusual beliefs have been perpetuated over the years. Loose clothing for men is thought to be more Muslim than the tight trousers worn by infidels. Some houses are thought of as being possessed by spirits because the inhabitants are constantly getting sick. Evil spirits are chased away with special ceremonies at the time the work on a new house is begun. The demand for blood vengeance by the next of kin of a slain man is universal in all Muslim countries including those of Southeast Asia. This vengeance can be settled by money rather than by blood (Hurgronje, 1906: I, 25, 43, 47).

The prayer at sunset is considered more important than the other four prayers. At Ramadan, prayers are offered by the Muslims more faithfully than during the rest of the year. Also during Ramadan, most of the devout Muslims fast in the daylight hours. Some fast only on the first day; others on the first and last; and still others on the first, last, and middle. Services are held in the mosque every night in Ramadan. *Slametans*, special cere-

---

12. "All Souls' Day" is a festival among the Maranao Muslims of the Philippines. Graves *(kobor)* of the honored dead are cleaned and lamps are lighted on them. A feast is prepared in which family and friends partake. This festival is distinct from All Saints' Day (November 1), which is widely observed by Christian Filipinos.

monial meals, are sometimes held in the mosque at Ramadan. This is to seek a blessing for participants or specified persons.

An unusually large number of Muslims from Southeast Asia make the annual pilgrimage to Mecca. Some of them save for years in order to finance such a trip. In Indonesia the government supports around 10,000 pilgrims in their expenses for making the pilgrimage each year. Thus a major influence in Malay Islam is the large number from this area who have become *hadjis*. On their return from Mecca the *hadjis* become missionaries and reformers to help bring Islam more into accord with the practice and teachings of what they have seen and heard in Mecca. This has removed some of the pagan elements from Islam in the Indonesian archipelago.

> If there is indifference as regards the *salat,* this is more than counterbalanced by the superabundant zeal for the *Hadjj,* for few parts of the Mohammedan world send so large a proportion of their population on this pilgrimage or bring so much wealth year by year to the holy cities of Arabia as the East Indian archipelago. (Hurgronje, 1906: II, 305)

The *hadji* in Malay Southeast Asia is considered a holy man and is respected by the Muslim people. He becomes a factor in the spread and strengthening of Islam in his area. A common Philippine belief is that once a person makes the trip to Mecca, he will then undergo a complete change from his past life and will from that time on be completely honest and just in all of his dealings with his fellow men, especially his fellow Muslims.

A detailed study by Gottfried Simon indicates that the Muslim Bataks in northern Sumatra are taught ten religious duties that are considered to be a part of the true faith. A man must show love to God; love to angels; love to the Qur'an; love to the prophets; love to the Muslim teachers; hatred to all the enemies of God (with the explanation that God hates all who are not Muslims); fear of the wrath of God; belief in the mercy of God; reverence and awe for the name Mecca, because Mecca is a holy name; a heart turned away from all that is contrary to God. Five things are taught as being well-pleasing to God: to go to the mosque and to pray there in Arabic; to teach the commandments of God; to devote one's energies to making other Muslims; to increase in virtue; and in humility.

The following ten items are displeasing to God: to pray without mentioning one's father and mother; to step over a grave without saying a prayer; to go abroad and not worship in a mosque; to travel with friends without asking their names and places of origin; not to keep an agreement; when reading the Qur'an to stop short of 100 verses; to speak in the presence of a Muslim teacher; to visit mosques without worshiping there; to give one's companion nothing when one has plenty of food; to make fun of the Muslim teacher or ruler.

Ten things are listed that destroy true faith: to have more than one God; to love evil; to do wrong to one's fellow believers; to quarrel with one's fellow believers; to think lightly of the ten parts essential to true belief; not to be afraid of losing one's faith; to copy the dress of unbelievers, for example a sun hat or necktie; not to believe in the mercy of God; to wear trousers of European manufacture; not to turn toward Mecca at prayer.

Finally there are eight things that must be avoided at all costs on one's deathbed: to destroy the religion of a fellow-believer; not to pray in Arabic; not to be afraid of everlasting torment; to cling to earthly riches; hatred; boasting; lying; to revile a teacher (Simon, 1912: 173, 174).

Walter Bonar Sidjabat, an Indonesian Christian theologian who has made a careful study of Islam in Indonesia, comes to the following conclusion about Indonesian Islam:

> It is true that there is a prevailing element of syncretism and mysticism in Indonesian Islam; but above all, the absolute unity of God to the Muslims means that Allah is the sole, personal and complete manifestation of the divine as revealed to the prophet Muhammad. . . . Yet it is clear then to all but the orthodox minority that belief in Allah is fused with the worship of all sorts of supernatural influences and forces, personified or not, which are indispensable to communal life. But one thing is sure that for a Muslim, whether his religious assumptions are based on orthodox principles or grounded on a syncretistic religious view, his faith in Allah is an absolute conviction. (Sidjabat, 1965: 54)

5 Islamic Resurgence Among Malay Muslims

A. Global View of Islamic Resurgence

In the Introduction a brief reference was made to the worldwide phenomenon called "Islamic Resurgence." It is also known as "Islamic Revival"[1] or

1. At a consultation of Christian and Muslim Asian scholars held in Singapore in 1980, the following description of "Islamic Revival" was issued by the Christian Conference of Asia (CCA). The theme of the consultation was "Islam's Challenge for Asian Churches."

Islamic Revival
  a. Islamic revival is concerned about the secularism and nationalism and atheistic beliefs and values that it sees in the West.
  b. Islamic revival seeks to make the Muslim a better Muslim through a return to Islamic teaching and practice based on the Qur'an. This call is *da'wa* or mission.
  c. Islamic revival emphasizes the universal *ummah,* worldwide Islamic community, where every Muslim lives according to *shariah* (Islamic law), concerned with justice and mercy.
  d. In Asia Muslims want not only an Islamic society but also an Islamic state. Back to Medina — the original Islamic community where minorities (non-Muslims) become second-class citizens.
  e. Islamic revival presents itself as a third way between western-style materialistic capitalism and atheistic communism, claiming that Islamic society will promote justice (Yap, 1980: 42).

"Islamic Renewal." Perhaps this development in the fifteenth century of Islam could be compared to the sixteenth-century Reformation of the church, which was a similar effort to return to the basic teachings and practice of the early Christian church. In the Reformation the emphasis was placed on the Holy Scripture as the only source of teaching and practice for the church. In Islamic Resurgence the emphasis is placed on the Qur'an and Hadith[2] as the only source of teaching and practice in Islam.

In recent years, we have seen a rash of newspaper headlines and magazine articles with such titles as "Islam on the March," "Living with Islam," "Islam and the West," "The Fundamental Fear," "Not Again, For Heaven's Sake," "Islamic Fundamentalism," "Militant Islam," "The Next War, They Say," and "A Holy War Heads West." All of these are indications that there is something exciting, something disturbing happening in the Muslim world. This is evidence that "Islamic Resurgence" is a reality in the entire Muslim world, and it causes many in the West to ask, "Will Islam replace Communism as the greatest threat to stability in the free world in the twenty-first century?" From the Muslim point of view, the question is asked, "Is the West the greatest threat to Islam in the fifteenth Islamic century?"[3]

Since the 1970s, the world has become aware of the presence and activity of Islam and Muslims. Although some people may still refer to the followers of Muhammad as Mohammedans, others who are more perceptive have noticed the change in spelling from Moslem to Muslim, from Koran to Qur'an. Islam and Muslims remain in the news and will continue to attract the attention of the rest of the world in the new millennium.

It should also be mentioned that, along with political resurgence and reformation, Islam has become an international missionary religion. In the West, Islam has found a positive response in Europe and North America. While Christian missionary activity is prohibited or severely restricted in

2. *Hadith* — an Arabic term referring to reports of words and actions from the life of Muhammad or his early successors called *Caliphs*.

3. "The myth of the monolith" demonstrates the wide diversity in Islam, including degrees and types of Islamic developments in recent years. These differences have caused misunderstanding and confusion among Western scholars and people in the West who consider Islam to be united and homogenous. This has resulted in a negative public image of Muslims and Islam even among those who are sympathetic to Muslim concerns (Ayoob, 1981: 18).

Muslim-controlled areas and countries, Muslims are free to seek converts without restriction in democratic societies.

In one sense, it can be documented that Islamic resurgence or "rising again" began over 200 years ago after centuries of decline and stagnation. The Wahabi Movement with the emphasis on return to classical Islam began in Saudi Arabia, the homeland of Islam, in the eighteenth century. The Sanusiyyah reform movement started in Algeria in the nineteenth century. At the same period of history, Jamal al-Din al-Afghani and Muhammad Abduh of Egypt were emphasizing the need to reform Islam. These reform movements were very different, but all had the same goal of purifying Islam (Muzaffar, 1987: 149, 150).

If the basic meaning of resurgence is "rising again," this implies that previously something has reached the heights. It also implies that following success, there was a decline and plunge to the depths. In its first seven centuries (A.D. 700-1400/A.H. 0-700), Islam sprang out of the Arabian Desert and conquered a large portion of the world. This was followed by five centuries of decline and loss (A.D. 1500-2000/A.H. 800-1400) when Islam was under the hegemony of Western European Christian nations. Now, many Muslim scholars argue that Islam is on the rise in its fifteenth century and ready not only to regain its past glory and political influence, but also to increase its influence over the entire world.

Islamic resurgence means a return to authentic Islamic practices and faith by following the Qur'an and Hadith. Sharia (Islamic law) will be the law of the land. Islamic resurgence will increase the dar-al-Islam (household of Islam) and decrease the opposition in the dar-al-harb (household of war). This requires jihad (struggle for the faith) and da'wa (mission to the world). The ultimate goal of resurgence is to bring the whole world under the controlling influence of Islam.

On the individual or personal level, resurgence also requires wearing of appropriate clothing modeled after the Arabs for both male and female. It means modeling daily life after the Prophet Muhammad — the perfect example for every Muslim. Resurgence means faithful, regular, five-times-a-day prayer at the mosque and memorizing the Arabic Qur'an. The once-in-a-lifetime *hajj* (pilgrimage to Mecca) becomes a top priority. Resurgence emphasizes that all Muslims are members of a universal community — *ummah*. In this *ummah* all Muslims will "enjoin what is right and forbid what is wrong and believe in God," based on the Qur'anic injunction (Sura 3: 104, 110). Some Muslims teach that *khalifah* means the authority to rule over the whole world and that *allah* (God) has given this power to the *ummah* (Safie, 1981: 73).[4]

In spite of the many common themes, emphases, and goals of Islamic resurgence, it takes different forms and approaches in different nations and cultures in the Muslim world. There are truly both a unity and diversity in Islam. In the following sections, Islamic resurgence will be examined among the Malay Muslims in Indonesia, Malaysia, and the Philippines.

The Malay Muslims of Southeast Asia were acutely aware of the international resurgence of Islam beginning with the 1973 Arab-Israeli War. This was followed by the worldwide oil embargo of the late 1970s implemented by the oil-rich Arab Muslim nations. Most Muslims were thrilled to see the Islamic Revolution in which the small Muslim nation of Iran stood up to the most powerful nation in the world, the United States of America. This was followed by the Soviet invasion of Afghanistan during which the *mujahadin* warriors provided a real challenge for the world's strongest Communist nation, the Soviet Union. All of these world-shaking events raised the hopes and consciousness of Muslims throughout the world. All agreed that Islam was becoming a major player in the world by rising again (Mutalib, 1990: 154).

B. Islamic Resurgence in Indonesia

Resurgence in Indonesia has taken a more subdued course than in other parts of the Malay world. Two Indonesian Christian scholars report that resurgence of Islam in Indonesia started at the beginning of the twentieth century. This resurgence was influenced by the Islamic modernist movement that had begun as Muslim reform in the Middle East. It was a contin-

---

4. A Muslim scholar, Mohammad Aziz Ahmad, made the following comment on Islam and politics:

> "Islam is religion" is the general view and "religion is politics." Religion and politics cannot be separated in Islam. A true Muslim is shocked to think in terms of religion and politics; he only thinks in terms of Islam. Islam is not only a religion or a name for beliefs or certain forms of worship, it is, in fact, a way of life — a complete code of guidance of the individual's entire life. . . . The Holy Qur'an lays down the broad principles of life. Islam is all embracing in its nature and affects all aspects of human activity of the people, of the country, and of humanity. (Ibrahim bin Safie, 1981: 73)

uation of the eighteenth-century Wahabiya movement in Saudi Arabia. In Indonesia this modernist movement resulted in the formation of two organizations. The *Sirikat Islam* (Islamic Union) was established in 1911 as an Islamic political group. In 1912 the *Muhammadijah* became an educational organization to promote Islamic life and practice through educational institutions. Thus, Muhammadijah made every effort to promote the modernist Islamic way of life and, at the same time, to oppose Dutch colonialism. Muhammadijah spread propaganda based on the Qur'an and Hadith to purify Islam from the influence of local tradition *(adat)* and mystical practices of Sufism.

Muhammadijah claimed that the weakness of Muslims in facing Western civilization was due to the irrational characteristics of Indonesian Islam and the influence of Sufism, which deviated from authentic Islamic practice. Muhammadijah was warmly welcomed among Muslim intellectuals and the general public in urban areas. It was successful in both promoting Muslim life and in opposing Dutch colonialism (Sitompul and Widdwissoeli, 1991: 2). Muhammadijah later evolved into a revivalist function through education and social welfare. The emphasis shifted to non-political Western modernization and Islamic modernism. The appeal of Islam was enhanced by the condemnation of materialism in the West (von der Mehden, 1986: 229, 230).

During the Japanese occupation of Indonesia in World War II, Muslim resistance helped to increase Muslim political influence, which continued in the struggle for independence from the Dutch after the war. The Dutch policy had been neutral toward the practice and spread of Islam in Indonesia, but the Dutch discouraged any Muslim political activity before World War II. Since the period of Dutch colonialism up to the present, efforts to keep Muslims from controlling the government have been successful under Sukarno and Suharto. It appears that the same policies of a secular government with some Islamic influence will continue following the 1999 elections in Indonesia.

"One problem was that if nothing unites Indonesia like Islam, neither does anything divide it so deeply" (McVey, 1983: 200). This observation of a Western scholar refers to the deep divisions in Indonesian Islam. Not only does Indonesia have over 300 ethnic groups with about 50 different languages, there are deep divisions in Islam: divisions between "modernists" and "traditionalists"; between *santri* and *abangan*. These divisions, according to Ruth McVey, mean that even though Indonesia is identified as the "world's largest Muslim nation, unambiguous Islam is a minority religion" (1983: 201). Due to restrictions on Islamic political parties, Muslim leaders have not participated in political activities. Thus, the Muhammadijah movement has emphasized its exclusive function as *da'wa*, meaning internal and external missionary activity through non-political social and welfare work.

In the Sukarno period after independence (1956-1965), "Guided Democracy" was implemented during which the military was the most powerful political force. The government was secular, with a common ideology that promoted Islamic practice according to military approval, and it succeeded in controlling the Muslim leaders who wanted to make an Islamic state. The role of the army changed after 1966 under the New Order of President Suharto. The army proposed and administered national policy with an emphasis on development. Suharto declared in 1972, "Religion will also return to its real function — providing a thorough teaching for life and development." This meant that religion would not have political power. This was a continuation of the policy implemented during the long period of Dutch colonialism (Federspiel, 1973: 407-10).

Indonesia has no viable Islamic political party and none has been allowed to be established.

> Unlike Malaysia, where Islamic resurgence and a strong Islamic party have led the government to embark on its own Islamic process, the Indonesian government goes all out to suppress any politicization of Islam and has no intention of meeting the demands of Muslims caught up in this religious fervor. (Tamara, 1986: 5)

In this way Indonesia has minimized the influence of resurgence in politics. There was one extreme example of an attempt to establish an Islamic state led by S. M. Kartosowirjo. Based in eastern Java, he led an armed struggle under the banner of *dar'ul Islam* from 1948 to 1962. The rebellion started under the Dutch and continued after independence. It ended in September 1962, when Kartosowirjo was executed for rebellion. It has also been reported that since 1983 the army under General Murdoni has been responsible for killing hundreds of Muslim fundamentalists (Das, 1987: 239). Thus, the Indonesian government has been deadly serious in keeping Islam out of politics. Nevertheless, Islamic resurgence has had a profound influence in Indonesia and has resulted in leading many Muslims to be more committed to Islam. Many new books on Islam are available in *bahasa Indonesia*. These books deal with Islamic society and state, economics, and justice (Tamara, 1986: 6).

One distinctive characteristic of the resurgence of Islam in Indonesia has been the strengthening and deepening of the religious nature of Islam. This includes the building of many mosques and the publishing and distribution of Islamic literature. Second, Islam is seeking some way to play a larger role in political decisions. Third, many Muslims have been concerned about the growth of the church in some parts of Indonesia. Fourth, Islam is becoming more involved in the social problems of Muslims (Bakker, 1972: 126-35). Islamic resurgence in Indonesia is more concerned with poverty and justice, while in Malaysia resurgence stresses Malay Muslim identity. As we will learn, the Philippine resurgence has led to armed struggle. This has not happened in Indonesia or Malaysia (Muzaffar, 1987: 157).

One interesting facet of the Islamic resurgence in Indonesia and throughout the Muslim world has been that there is no question about the belief in God, *Allah* in the Arabic language. All Muslims continue to believe in God. The Indonesian Muslim may be lax in the practice of Islam in daily life, but he is fiercely loyal to Islam and desires to remain a Muslim.

The national ideology of Indonesia, called *panca sila* (five principles), was implemented under President Sukarno in 1945 and continues up to the present time. The first of these five principles is simply "belief in one God." This is acceptable to Christians and other religious minorities of Indonesia — Hindu, Buddhists, *kepercayaan* (Javanese Mysticism). "Belief in one God," however, is not completely satisfactory to conservative Muslims, who have made several official attempts to add the words, "with the obligation for Muslims to observe Islamic law." These attempts have failed so far. The Javanese *abangan* who are not fully committed to Islam and secular-oriented Muslims have strongly opposed the establishment of an Islamic state. The first two Indonesian presidents, Sukarno and Suharto, both came from the Javanese abangan community (Crouch, 1988: 191).

During the 1970s, Islamic resurgence was evident in Indonesia. While the government continued the policy of not allowing Islam to be involved in policy-making, at the same time the government officially encouraged and promoted Islam in social, educational, and religious activities. This has served to strengthen Islam and has led many Muslims to a better understanding and more faithful practice of Islam (Anwar, 1979: 100). There is no doubt that this greater commitment to Islam will lead to greater interest and involvement in political activity and decision-making. If the trend continues, it is possible that Indonesia, along with Malaysia, may become an Islamic state with a dominating influence in Malay Southeast Asia (Hefner, 1987: 549).

During the 1970s and 1980s Islamic radicals in Indonesia were actively involved in the plan to establish an Islamic state. One group, called the Indonesian Revoluters Board, was reported to be asking assistance from Iran to overthrow the Suharto government. In 1985 Islamic radicals destroyed shopping malls, claiming they were non-Islamic. There were riots and bombings at the ancient Borobudur Buddhist shrine near Jogjakarta. These incidents were blamed on Islamic radicals (von der Mehden, 1986: 226).

Another facet of resurgence in Indonesia is Islamic modernism, with its attempt to find an alternative to materialistic capitalism and atheistic communism. This third way is to be based on Islamic principles and Indonesian culture.

> The movement of an alternative Muslim development must begin as a cultural movement that liberates human beings from the status of commodity fetishism, to use a word from Marx himself. In addition, it is liberty from tyranny and exploitation of man or institutions through the use of the Qur'an. (Tamara, 1986: 8, 9)

One of the significant emphases of resurgent Islam in Indonesia is the decrease in fascination with the western world. An effort is made to find solutions in Islam; Western societies do not have answers to Indonesian problems. Intellectuals and others are asking if the answer to inequality, economic crisis, unemployment, etc., can be found in Islam (Tamara, 1986: 9). Discussions on Islam are held in mosques and are well attended. The participants are mostly students and other youth. The mosque in Bandung has been a popular venue for these discussions. Bandung is a good barometer of the Indonesian political climate and has been called "one of the centres of Islamic revival in Indonesia." Many young people from Djakarta have attended a three-day "mental training" course at the Bandung mosque at the Institute of Technology (the alma mater of President Sukarno). This course was taught by Imaduddin, who at one time was sentenced to one year in prison. His teaching continues through his students to promote a rational Islam. The debate about Islam and politics in Indonesia does not take place in public but in small groups, mainly among intellectuals. This debate does not reach the masses; thus, the full effect of Islamic resurgence is difficult to measure in Indonesia (Tamara, 1986: 6-9).

Many agree that Indonesia must become an Islamic state, but they do not agree on how to reach that goal. Other Indonesian Muslims prefer the *status quo* with the separation of religion and politics. The latter view prevails at the present time with no realistic possibility of drastic change at the beginning of the twenty-first century (Tamara, 1986: 9). The majority of Indonesia's Muslims prefer a democratic system over a theocratic Iranian model. Most Indonesian Muslims see religion as an individual concern; at the same time, they believe that Islam should be propagated and taught extensively. How long will this moderate view prevail in Indonesia? It is impossible to determine an answer at this time. As the Islamization of Indonesia with the increasing influence of the global Islamic resurgence continues, more and more Indonesian Muslims will fully understand and practice Islamic teaching. Then the possibility of an Islamic state can become a reality.

C. Islamic Resurgence in Malaysia

In the early part of the twentieth century, Islamic resurgence had reached to the Malay Muslims of Southeast Asia. While Malaysia was still under the British rule, the call was heard to return to the Qur'an and *Sunnah*[5] (Muzaffar, 1987: 151). This followed the general pattern of Islamic resurgence, which also required all Muslims to reject worldly habits such as gambling and drinking alcoholic beverages. It always included the mandate to "return to Islamic living" and the rejection of Western moral values.

Since the end of World War II, the newly independent nations of Malay Southeast Asia have been led by political secularists who were opposed to the political influence of conservative religious leaders in their respective nations — namely, Indonesia, Malaysia, and the Philippines. This led to different responses to Islamic resurgence in these countries.

A respected Malaysian Muslim scholar of Indian, not Malay, heritage offers the following complete definition of Islamic resurgence:

5. *Sunnah* — an example from the life of the Prophet Muhammad as found in the *hadith*. About 90 percent of Muslims follow sunnah, thus the name "sunni."

Islamic resurgence is a description of the endeavor to re-establish Islamic values, Islamic practices, Islamic institutions, Islamic laws, indeed Islam in its entirety, in the lives of Muslims everywhere. It is an attempt to re-create an Islamic ethos, an Islamic social order in the vortex of which is the Islamic human being, guided by the Qur'an and the Sunnah. (Muzaffar, 1987: 2)

A Western scholar has identified four groups involved in Islamic resurgence or revival in Indonesia and Malaysia. These four groups are classified as: traditionalists, radicals, fundamentalists, and revivalists. Each group has received different response from the different governments. Malaysia, with 52 percent Malay Muslim population, necessarily makes a different response to resurgence than Indonesia, which has an almost 90 percent Muslim population (von der Mehden, 1986: 219).

While Malaysia is not an Islamic state, Islam is the official national religion. The Muslim population consists of three groups. First are the secularly educated middle class; second are the Islamic-educated teachers and civil servants. The first group adheres to Western norms and values while the second is resolved to follow Islamic moral and political values (Ibrahim bin Safie, 1981: 77). The third and largest group are the working class, with little formal education and low incomes (Muzaffar, 1987: 154, 155).

The "traditionalists" in Malaysia include the vast majority of Malay Muslims living in small villages. These traditionalists are more of a potential threat than a present danger in the political arena. Nevertheless, the two major political parties are seeking the support of the traditionalists.

The "fundamentalist" Muslims are similar to fundamentalist Christians. They both seek a return to the roots to practice the "pure" religion of the original founders. Malay Muslim fundamentalists promote the conservative, orthodox interpretation of Islam. They want an Islamic state based on the Qur'an and Hadith. They wish to suppress and reject technology and "western" influence. The leaders are found in the local *ulama*[6] and Islamic schools as well as in *da'wa*[7] groups. They encourage wearing of Arab

---

6. *Ulama* (singular *alim*) are considered to be religious scholars in Islam, similar to clergy in the church.

7. *Da'wa* — also transliterated from the Arabic as *dahwah* or *dakwah*. Da'wa is comparable to mission in the church. It is a "call" to follow Islam, and is used not only for

clothing for both sexes. The Malaysian government considers the fundamentalists as a real threat to their policies of development and democracy. The Chinese and Indian minorities, especially the Christians, see the fundamentalists as a divisive threat to national unity, progress, and stability (von der Mehden, 1986: 223, 224).

The "radicals" are more extreme in their rhetoric and action than the conservatives. They, at times, resort to violence to promote their demands for a strictly Islamic state. In Malaysia in the late 1970s they made a series of attacks on Hindu temples as the "Army of Allah." In the 1980s the radicals continued the attempt to purify the country and to establish an Islamic state. They have even been suspected and accused of plotting the assassination of cabinet members. The Malaysian government has used the violence perpetrated by the radicals as justification to control and restrict nonviolent activities of the traditionalists and fundamentalists when they oppose government policy or development (von der Mehden, 1986: 226, 227).

The "revivalists" are those Malay Muslim teachers and scholars who seek to adapt Islam to the modern situation. They emphasize the importance of preaching Islam among the faithful. They also encourage Muslims to learn modern technological skills. They profess to be non-political and emphasize education, economic progress, and da'wa activities. They stress a stricter adherence to Islam and promote social and economic issues.

One organization that serves as an example of revivalists in Malaysia is the youth group, ABIM (Angkazan Bolia Islam Malaysia), which stresses education, Islamic identity, and understanding among Muslims. ABIM also gives top priority to first Islamicizing the *ummah*. ABIM leadership has encouraged a pluralistic society in Malaysia where social justice includes all religious groups (von der Mehden, 1986: 227, 228). ABIM has called on the government to implement *shariah* (Islamic law) to create a just society.

A respected member of the *ulama* in Indonesia notes that Islam has gone into decline only when it has failed to practice Islamic teaching. He declares that not only can Islam overcome its backwardness and underdevelopment of many Muslim countries, but Islam can be a positive, driving force in encouraging and promoting development. He states that this positive Islamic response has been adopted by the leaders in Malaysia. He

---

gaining new converts, but to revive or reform the faith and life of all Muslims, especially lapsed Muslims.

firmly believes that Islam will be better understood and accepted if it adjusts to technological change. In this way, Islam will also be a strong force against communism (Hamka, 1978: 223).[8] Tun Abdul Razak, as Deputy Prime Minister in 1963, emphasized the need for Malay Muslims to modernize their thinking. He stressed two aspects of Islam. First, *ta'abbudi* concerns duties to God, while *ta'aqquli* is concerned with the use of logic and human wisdom.

The current Islamic resurgence in Malaysia was introduced in the late 1970s by the *jamaat tableegh*,[9] based in India, and the *dar'ul argam*,[10] a local Malay organization. At the beginning, Indian and Pakistani Muslims residing in Malaysia were active in Tableegh, but gradually Malays became dominant. They propagated their fundamentalist ideology at the grassroots level.

A more influential group of Malay resurgents were college youth educated in both English and Malay. They became involved in various universities in Malaysia and overseas, especially England, where they were on government scholarships. These university students and graduates formed a strong attachment to Islam plus a fervent desire to lead an Islamic revival in Malaysia. Many of these youth were active in the formation of ABIM,[11] which established an aggressive da'wa program. As students returned from overseas, they became involved in the Islamization of Malay society (Bakar, 1981: 1041-44).

8. Hamka is the *nom de plume* for Professor Dr. Haji Abdulmalik bin Abdulkatism bin Amrullah, who has written more than 300 published works. He organized opposition against Sukarno in Indonesia and was involved in several Islamic organizations.

9. *Jamaat Tableegh* started as an Islamic da'wa movement in India in the 1920s. It found a ready following among the Indian Muslims in Malaysia in the 1950s. More recently, it has gained many followers from Malay Muslims, even in rural Malaysia. Tableegh favors the political status quo. It has also been active in Indonesia and the Philippines (*Third World Quarterly*, 1988: 845).

10. *Dar'ul Argam* was established in Malaysia in 1968 by twelve followers of Ustaz (Islamic scholar) Ashari Muhammad. It attracted many followers by emphasizing Islamic society as a first step toward an Islamic state. In the 1990s, the Malaysian government restricted the activities of Dar'ul Argam as "deviationist" (*TWQ*, 1988: 846).

11. ABIM — Angkazan Bolia Islam Malaysia was founded in 1971 by former members of the National Association of Malaysian Islam Students (PKPIM). Its main membership comes from youth in institutes of higher learning. In the early stages, ABIM's major goal, like PAS, was to establish an Islamic state. That goal has been modified in its association with UMNO (*TWQ*, 1988: 846).

These Malay Muslim youth considered Islamic resurgence/revival as the major ideology of dissent. They proposed a new framework for society built on Islamic principles and practice as follows:

1. Islam is a comprehensive way of life. Religion is integral to politics, state, law, and society.
2. Muslim societies fail because they depart from this understanding of Islam by following Western secular and materialistic ideologies and values.
3. Renewal calls for Islamic political and social revolution that draws inspiration from the Qur'an and from Muhammad, who led the first Islamic movement.
4. To re-establish God's rule, Western-imposed civil law must be replaced by Islamic law, which is the blueprint for Muslim society.
5. While Westernization of society is condemned, modernization as such is not. Science and technology are accepted, but they are to be subordinated to Islam in order to guard against the infiltration of Western values. (Anwar, 1987: 1, 2)

In addition to Tableegh, Dar'ul Argam and ABIM, there is a strong political party that advocates Islamic resurgence through the government. This is the Parti Islam Se Malaysia, usually referred to by the acronym PAS. PAS became the successor to the first political party of Islamic reformism, the *Hizbul Muslim,* which grew out of the MATA or Pan Malayan Islamic Council in 1949. PAS was influenced by Islamic reformism, Indonesian nationalism, a mild form of socialism, and a conservative defense of Malay rights (Funston, 1976: 58, 59). PAS was formed in 1951 by members who were dissatisfied with the ruling political party, the United Malay National Organization (UMNO).[12] PAS is based in the traditional, conservative Malay states among the rural population. PAS has combined Malay nationalism with the campaign to establish a Muslim state (Funston, 1976: 69, 73).

---

12. UMNO — The United Malay National Organization has dominated Malaysian politics since independence. It accomplished this by forming an alliance with the minority political parties — the Malaysian Chinese Association (MCA) and the Malaysian Indian Congress (MIC). In the 1980s the National Party, Barisan, was formed. Barisan consisted of UMNO, MCA, and MIC. For a while it also included PAS. After PAS broke away, UMNO attracted the leadership of ABIM (Nash, 1987: 567).

In order to lessen the threat of "militant" Islam from PAS and other re-surgent agendas, the Malaysian government under the majority UMNO leadership has continued to favor pro-Islamic policies and encouragement of Islamic practices. This has resulted in prejudice in favor of Islam and prejudice against the other religious minorities — Buddhist, Christian, Hindu, and Sikh. In favoring the Malay majority, the government has also discriminated against the Chinese and Indian minorities who make a sub-stantial economic contribution to Malaysia (Mutalib, 1990: 156).

The UMNO thinks it necessary to adopt a pro-Islamic stance due to the pressure from the pro-Islamic party PAS. Also, the Sultans who rule the fed-erated Malay state take a firm pro-Islamic stand since, according to the con-stitution, they are the guardians and "protectors of Malay culture and reli-gion." This is a heritage of the British colonial policy of non-interference in religion among the Malays. At the same time, the UMNO has had to place limits on some aspects of Islam to prevent Malaysia from becoming an Is-lamic state and establishing an Islamic social order. The government has tried to maintain a multi-racial Malaysia based on equity, justice, tolerance, and education. It is true that Islam is favored by the government, but Islam has not yet gained control of the government (Mutalib, 1990: 157).

Thus, there is an attempt by UMNO to walk a tightrope between Islam and Malay identity. In the fear that Islam would create instability and un-rest with the end of a multi-religious polity, the government exerts efforts to keep Islam from being mixed with politics. This often results in ambigu-ous policies in attempts to satisfy all parties. This usually satisfies no one.

The government has taken action when there is a threat from funda-mentalist Islam. In June 1994, Prime Minister Mahathir Muhammad an-nounced that Al-Argam had become a threat because its literature was propagating "deviationist" teachings. Since 1988 Al-Argam's founder and teacher, Ashari Muhammad, has been in self-exile (*Asiaweek*, 1994: 28).

Just like Islam in Indonesia, Islam in Malaysia has been a unifying and dividing force among Malay Muslims. Most Muslims in Malaysia wish to stress their identity as Malays. At the same time, they want to be identified with the Arab Muslim world. In 1984, Judith Nagata wrote a popular book entitled *Born Again Malay* (not Born Again Muslim!) to demonstrate the overwhelming emphasis on ethnic identity as Malays as a result of Islamic resurgence in Malaysia (Mutalib, 1990: 159).

The dominant type of Islam in Malaysia at the close of the twentieth century can be classified as "folk Islam," meaning it still has pre-Islamic elements. Thus, the Islamic "revival" or "resurgence" in Malaysia since the 1970s is more of increased religiosity than a practice of "high" or "classical" Islam. As one Malaysian religious leader commented on the situation among Malay Muslims, "There is no desire among the majority of Muslims for more Islamic laws." The da'wa organization has had little success in changing this attitude of the masses concerning their indifference or lack of interest in changing or improving Islamic practices. Even PAS has generally preferred traditional ethnic practice instead of Islamic standards.

It is interesting to note that long before it became enshrined in the constitution that "Malay means Muslim," it was already considered a part of the culture. The expression *"masok melayu"* in the language *bahasa melayu* has a double meaning: (1) "to convert to Islam" and (2) "to become a Malay." Thus, the emphasis on identity as Malay in preference to Muslim is not surprising (Israeli, 1982: 140).

Another more recent official definition states that a Malay is a person whose first (and often only) language is *bahasa melayu,* who follows the customs of the Malays . . . and who is a Muslim by faith. Furthermore, a constitutional Malay, as recognized by Malaysian law, is one whose parents have all the Malay characteristics (Nash, 1987: 562). Such a narrow definition of Malay is limited to the citizens of West Malaysia who occupy the Malay Peninsula. It does not include the millions of Malay Muslims, Christians, and animistic tribes living in the Indonesian Archipelago and the Philippine Islands.

The Islamic resurgence in Malaysia is also a basis for the Bumiputra/non-Bumiputra[13] dichotomy. Islam gives the Bumiputra an identity that is similar to the Malay/non-Malay dichotomy. Resurgence has given meaning and identity to the Muslim/non-Muslim division in Malaysia. Ethnic identity is protected by religion. Even those opposed to the Bumiputra/non-Bumiputra and Malay/non-Malay dichotomy are committed to the Muslim/non-Muslim identity for all citizens. This identity is almost interchangeable since all Malays are Muslims and the majority of Bumiputras are also Muslims (Muzaffar, 1987: 23-25).

Even before the full impact of Islamic resurgence began to influence Malay politics and religion, there was conflict and competition between

---

13. *Bumiputra* — A Malay term meaning "son of soil." It is used to mean the indigenous tribal groups of Malaysia who are offered special concessions and benefits by the government.

PAS and UMNO. PAS considers itself to be the only pure advocate of Islam while UMNO is "impure" and "contaminated." PAS points out that UMNO has failed to establish an Islamic state and has not implemented *shariah* (Muslim law);[14] therefore, PAS considers UMNO to be outside of Islam. PAS has gone so far as to call UMNO members "kafir" (unbelievers).

PAS also calls itself "the oppressed" who are under the "Oppressors." UMNO considers this PAS pressure as the reason that government policies must favor the Malay Muslims at the expense of inequity toward the religious and cultural minorities. The minorities are not always treated with justice and equality. These concerns and fears are increased when there are reliable reports of forced conversions to Islam of teenaged Chinese girls in several Malay states where PAS has a majority. The Muslim/non-Muslim tension is increased. Yet PAS continues to insist that an Islamic state would bring justice and happiness to all citizens of Malaysia. Such propaganda is rejected by both Muslims and non-Muslims (Muzaffar, 1987: 85-87).

A Muslim scholar predicts that polarization will continue to grow among Malay Muslims. The division is between "Islam from above" (the government) and "Islam from below" (the counter-elite). Chinese Malaysians also see the Islamization program of the government "as a deadly threat to their way of life." Can UMNO continue to control the Islamic resurgence or will the resurgence control the UMNO? The pressure keeps growing; small concessions to Islam only seem to increase the demand for more concessions (Ayoob, 1981: 99, 100).

Religious freedom, which is guaranteed by the Malaysian constitution, is under threat because of laws passed and proposed by parliament that favor Islam over the minority religions. This has resulted in the polarization of Malaysian society — both religious and racial polarization. For most citizens, the top priority is racial, not national identity. Thus, it means more to be Malay, Chinese, Indian, Kadzan, Iban, etc., than to be a Malaysian. Even more ominous than racial polarization is religious polarization, in which one religious group is strongly favored over the others. In the proposal for an Islamic state, it is clear that non-Muslim Malaysian citizens would have only an advisory status in the formation of national policies. They would be relegated to second-class citizenship. Such a development could disenfranchise almost half of Malaysia's population.

14. *Shariah* — the complete, comprehensive Islamic code of laws based on the Qur'an and hadith.

The UMNO has called itself the "protector of Islam." In opposition to PAS, UMNO claims to be the vehicle for Islamic values. The government under UMNO has promoted *da'wa,* established an Islamic bank and the International Islamic University, has been involved in international Muslim organizations and meetings, recognized Muslim holidays as national holidays, and increased programming and articles about Islam through all media. UMNO has not advocated an Islamic state; instead, it declares that Malaysia "already operates under the code and values of the Islamic faith" (von der Mehden, 1986: 230-32).

The governments of both Indonesia and Malaysia have adopted strategies to minimize the destabilizing effects of resurgence in the eighties and nineties. Tensions remain high between the government and those advocating an Islamic state. The problems created by resurgent Islam have not been solved, but they have been temporarily restricted. Islamic expectations will continue to cause tensions and possible conflict in the beginning of the twenty-first century (von der Mehden, 1986: 232-33).

The basic form of Islamic resurgence in Malaysia has been referred to as "ethnic Malay nationalism: This implies that it has been limited to the 52 percent Malay majority (Mutalib, 1990: 153). The Malays in Malaysia have supported the global Islamic resurgence with financial aid, demonstrations, and publicity. This has led to Malay interest in reforming Islam among the youth and the masses. Malaysian Muslim leaders in government promote stronger ties with other Muslim nations, especially the Gulf States. Many have begun to follow Islamic principles and even adopted Arab-style dress (Mutalib, 1990: 154, 155).

Even though ABIM generally followed a more moderate approach to Islamization than PAS, the UMNO considered ABIM to be a political threat, especially if ABIM formed an alliance with PAS. ABIM's leadership and members are university trained with knowledge of modern communications and organization. The UMNO pre-empted this threat by attracting the top ABIM leader, Anwar Ibrahim, to join UMNO as deputy prime minister, with the possibility of succeeding Mahathir as prime minister in the year 2000. This arrangement has changed in 1999 as Anwar Ibrahim has been accused of serious crimes by the prime minister. At the time of writing, this case is under appeal and a final decision has not been made. Many believe that Anwar Ibrahim will make a political recovery and lead Malaysia in the twenty-first century.

As the influence of Islam has increased among the masses in Malaysia, the UMNO has been able to contain the forces of fundamentalism and militant Islam by making concessions to Islam. At the present time there is no united, coherent Islamic opposition to UMNO. As long as the non-Muslim political parties continue to support UMNO, there is little possibility of an "Islamic revolution" in Malaysia similar to what happened in Iran. UMNO has shown its ability to manage the challenge of the Islamic resurgence while maintaining communal stability (Bakar, 1981: 1046, 1047; Mutalib, 1990: 161; Nash, 1987: 570).

What has been the response of the minority groups in Malaysia to the challenge of Malay Islamic resurgence? Interestingly, it has caused the minorities to return to their religious and cultural heritage. There has been a general religious and cultural revival and resurgence. Buddhist and Hindu communities in Malaysia are once again observing almost forgotten traditional religious festivals and rituals. Christians are rediscovering the role of Christ's example and teachings in their daily lives while seeking new converts from the non-Muslim population in the urban areas. The Chinese Malaysians are showing more determination to preserve their ancient culture and heritage. Thus, the Islamic resurgence has resulted in a resurgence and a renewed identity for all the minority communal groups in Malaysia.

The negative aspect of this renewed religious and cultural identity is a polarization along religious lines. There is very little social interaction among the different religious groups in Malaysia. Pride in one's own religion often results in ridicule of other religions. Religious polarization combined with ethnic polarization is a real threat to Malaysian unity, development, and economic stability. Such a situation places a dark cloud over Malaysia's future (Muzaffar, 1987: 98, 99).

A Malaysian Christian scholar and professor makes the following response to Islamic resurgence among the Malay Muslims of Malaysia:

> In 1993, the economic prospects for Malaysia were very optimistic (this was before the Asian economic setback of 1996). Prime Minister, Dr. Mahathir Mohammad, as head of UMNO and government was favoring Malay Muslims through social and economic policy (the New Economic Policy, NEP), thus laying the foundation for Islamic resurgence to increase in Malaysia. This included government support of material and spiritual growth of Malay Muslims while neglecting to encourage development of other ethnic and religious groups. (Batumalai, 1944)

Changes made in the constitution also favor Malay Muslims at the expense of other ethnic groups. This was not so severe as "ethnic cleansing," but it was surely "ethnic favoritism" at the expense of the minority ethnic groups. Some Malay Muslim leaders have opposed the policy of favoring Malay Muslims and advocate a pluralism in Malaysian politics in which all citizens are treated fairly and equally, instead of promoting Islamization through government policies.

In addition to the many Islamic institutions, and government support of Islam in favoring Islam as a national religion, severe restrictions and limitations have been placed on the activities of other religious groups. For example, there is limitation on the publication and distribution of Christian literature. A 1993 bill states that it is illegal for a Muslim to change his faith. There is nothing to restrict a conversion to Islam. A non-Muslim male cannot marry a Muslim female without first converting to Islam. It is difficult, if not impossible, for non-Muslim religious groups to obtain additional land for places of worship, schools, and cemeteries. It is difficult to obtain a visa for a visiting teacher or evangelist. Religious education is not offered for non-Muslims, yet they are required to study Islam. Rulings favoring Muslims are implemented with no concern for how they may affect others. It is against Malaysian law to write, speak, preach, or do anything against Muslim law. Some Malaysian laws are a violation of the United Nations Declaration of Human Rights which has been endorsed by Malaysia as a U.N. member.

Thus, the Islamic resurgence, together with the response of the Malaysian government, has limited the religious freedom and basic human rights of non-Muslims. There is a need to review and revise the Malaysian constitution to correct the erosion of fundamental rights of non-Muslim Malaysian citizens. This includes the Internal Security Act (ISA), the Printing Act, etc. There is an urgent need for all the citizens of Malaysia to work together for the good of the entire country. All citizens must have the same opportunities and rights. All citizens have the same responsibility to work together to alleviate poverty, disease, and ignorance. The Islamic resurgence can have a positive result for all citizens if it awakens each community to be sensitive to the needs and hopes of the other communities. The population is almost equally divided between Muslim and non-Muslims. It seems this is the appropriate time and place to put into practice the Quranic admonition paraphrased in English as follows:

"If there must be competition among you,
let it be competition in doing good."

D. Islamic Resurgence in the Philippines

The Spanish fought the Muslim Moro invaders of their Iberian homeland for over 700 years — from 711 A.D. until 1492 A.D., when they finally succeeded, at the Battle of Granada, in driving the Muslims out of Spain and back across the Strait of Gibraltar into North Africa. Then, as we learn in the history of the Spanish period of exploration and colonization, the Spanish ships reached the Pacific island chain they would name in honor of their young Prince Philip — the Philippines — in 1517. They established the first permanent Spanish colony in Cebu in 1565. There they discovered that their ancient enemy, the Moros, had arrived in Southeast Asia ahead of them. In 1578 A.D. Spain declared a resumption of war on the Muslims in the Philippines with the intention of conquering and converting them to the Christian faith. These "Moros Wars" continued until the end of the Spanish period in the Philippines in 1898. Thus the Spanish have the unenviable distinction of fighting against Muslims in Spain for 760 years and continuing to fight against the Muslims in the Philippines for an additional 320 years. At roughly a thousand years, this is the longest Christian-Muslim war in history! In the Philippines, Spain recruited Malay Christian converts to fight against their fellow Malay Muslims. Thus, it is not surprising to learn that there is a large residue of prejudice and mutual antipathy between the minority Muslim Filipinos and the majority Christian Filipinos that persists in various forms and actions at the end of the twentieth century.

The United States of America took control of the Philippines from the Spanish in 1898 as a result of the Spanish-American War that started in Cuba. After a few one-sided battles, the American military gained control of the Muslim areas in western Mindanao and Sulu. They did not try to convert the Muslims by force as the Spanish had done. They treated the Muslims fairly and established civil government with schools, hospitals, and infrastructure in the Muslim areas. In 1935, when the U.S. announced its intent to grant independence to the Philippines, Muslim Filipino leaders drew up a petition to the U.S. government, requesting that the Muslim minority areas remain under control of the U.S. rather than being placed under the majority Christian Filipino government. This request was denied, and the American government implemented a policy of integration of Muslims into the Christian Filipino society. A "Moro Province," consisting of Mindanao and Sulu, was created and placed under the supervision of Christian Filipinos just before World War II (Noble, 1984: 43). The Japanese army occupied the Philippines from 1942 to 1945. Both Christian and Muslim Filipinos collaborated to resist and fight against the Japanese in guerrilla action until the end of the war.

Despite the devastation and destruction of the Philippines at the end of the war, the U.S. kept its promise to grant independence to the Republic of the Philippines on July 4, 1946. In addition to all the economic, political, and social problems, the new government of the Republic of the Philippines (GRP) inherited the "Moro Problem" — also known as the "Muslim Problem" or the "Mindanao Problem." This problem received a very low priority in the list of many more urgent national problems. The GRP continued to follow the American policy of "integration," which was anathema to the perceptive Muslim. Integration implied the Muslim was to become just like the Christian Filipino. For the Muslim this meant "assimilation" or "conversion" with the denial and loss of Muslim identity. This was totally unacceptable to faithful Muslims, especially with the new winds of Islamic resurgence blowing into the southern Philippines in the 1950s. Muslim teachers from Saudi Arabia, Egypt, and Pakistan visited the Muslim areas in Mindanao and Sulu; they saw the need to promote Islamization in all these Muslim areas. Muslim Filipino leaders encouraged them to stay and help. The masses considered them to be "holy men" who had come to teach them more orthodox Islam than the "folk Islam" of their ancestors.

A traditional Muslim Filipino from one of the prominent Maranao families — the late, former Senator Domacao Alonto — deserves much credit for introducing Islamic renewal or resurgence in the Philippines. He traveled to the major Muslim Filipino areas to stress the need for reform of Islam. He translated the Qur'an into the Maranao language. Senator Alonto also visited the Malay Muslims in Indonesia and Malaysia to enlist their support in helping Muslim Filipinos to become better Muslims. He established the *Ansar al-Islam* among Maranao Muslim youth, and it spread to other areas in the Philippines. Senator Alonto also visited the Middle East and requested teachers to come to the Philippines. He established the first Muslim College in Marawi City, a college that continues to the present time (Ayoob, 1981: 218). Other Muslim Filipino leaders went to study Islam in Saudi Arabia, Egypt, and Pakistan. They returned to the Philippines to establish and teach in Muslim schools in the urban areas of Mindanao and Sulu (Majul, 1985: 35).

In the 1960s, high schools were built in most of the Muslim villages in the Muslim areas of Mindanao and Sulu. These schools were given Arabic names, but many of them were poor quality with unqualified teachers and few textbooks. It seemed that many of these schools were motivated by profit more than by the teachings of the Prophet. During these years I personally distributed hundreds of used textbooks, which were donated from the U.S., to many of the schools in the Lake Lanao area. I also established a student center in downtown Marawi City which had a fairly good library that was used often by students of various schools in Marawi.

Another evidence of Islamic resurgence among the Malay Muslims of the southern Philippines was the building of mosques in all the Muslim villages. In the Lake Lanao area it seemed that the Maranaos had an ongoing competition as to which village could build the best mosque. It was during this period that the architecture of the mosque changed from the roof with pagoda style to the inverted onion-shaped cupola. Also, there was the subtle change from using the drum for the call to prayer to using recordings over loudspeakers, sometimes with the voice of a *muezzin* chanting the *adhan*.[15] The drum was thought to be "non-Islamic."

Most of the activities in the 1950s in the Muslim areas of the southern Philippines might better be referred to as "awakening" rather than "resurgence." The Muslim Filipino was awakening to the reality that he was living in the independent Republic of the Philippines with a large Christian majority. He was also awakening to the awareness that he was part of a larger Malay Muslim community in neighboring Indonesia and Malaysia. This Malay Muslim community was an integral part of the universal Muslim community — the *ummah*. This was reinforced by the thousands of Muslim Filipinos going to Mecca every year. Thus, this period of the fifties and sixties was the beginning of a peaceful resurgence among Muslim Filipinos. The self-identity of most was "Muslim" or "Maranao" or "Tao-Sug." Very few Muslims would refer to themselves as "Filipino" because, to them, the first meaning of Filipino was "Christian."

---

15. *Adhan* — the Muslim call to prayer in the Arabic language, sounded five times a day from the mosque. *Muezzin* — the person who issues the *adhan*, the call to prayer five times a day. Sometimes the adhan is from a recording over a loudspeaker.

In this period of increasing recognition of Muslim identity among Muslim Filipinos, there was the general feeling that they could not fully practice their Muslim way of life in the Philippines' Christian-dominated system. The Islamic resurgence also led to a greater suspicion of both Christians and the West. There were more and more Christian Filipinos moving into the unoccupied agricultural lands in Mindanao, especially in the Maguindanao area of Cotabato. There were no Christian immigrants in the Maranao area around Lake Lanao.

A tragic incident in early 1968 turned the peaceful resurgency into a violent Muslim insurgency — the "Corregidor Massacre." A full explanation of the background of this incident has never been made public. Both Christian and Muslim Filipinos were incensed to learn that at least thirty-eight young Muslim soldiers were executed by the Philippine military in March 1968. These soldiers were in training for guerrilla warfare under the name of Jabidah Commandos. This was said to be for secret infiltration into Sabah in North Borneo, a state of East Malaysia. Since 1962, the Philippines had claimed that Sabah was part of the Philippines, formerly under the Sultan of Sulu. Malaysia strongly opposed this claim. One version explains that when the "Jabidah Commandos" learned the purpose of their training, they rebelled and refused to fight against their fellow Malay Muslims in Sabah. Thus the military silenced them by killing them. This caused Malaysia to protest to the GRP. It caused Muslim Filipinos to doubt if they could ever trust the GRP (Gowing, 1979[b]: 191, 192; Ayoob, 1981: 218).

The Corregidor Massacre was followed by the establishment of the Muslim (later Mindanao) Independence Movement (MIM) in Cotabato in May 1968. The MIM Manifesto demanded a separate Islamic state of Mindanao and Sulu. This was followed by several violent clashes between Maguindanao Muslims and Christian immigrants in Cotabato. Battles between Muslim "Blackshirts" of MIM and Christian Ilagas (rats) in Cotabato and Lanao del Norte were reported. This was the beginning of a shooting war in Mindanao with the Christian civilians being assisted by the Philippine army and constabulary. Many Muslim and Christian farmers, who were caught in the crossfire, abandoned their farms and evacuated their families to safe places (Ayoob, 1981: 218, 219). These incidents brought the "Muslim problem" to the headlines of Manila and international newspapers. It also made the "Muslim problem" a higher priority of the GRP.

There were constant rumors about a Muslim Secessionist Movement in early 1970. Muslim youth were said to be receiving months of rigid military training in the Middle East and Malaysia. The GRP tried to bring the situation under control by sending more troops to Mindanao and Sulu. The fighting continued and spread to new areas.

On September 21, 1972, President Marcos proclaimed martial law to oppose the Muslim rebellion in the southern Philippines and the Communist rebellion in the north. One month later Muslim rebels attacked the military camp in Marawi City and gained control of the campus and radio station at Mindanao State University. An appeal was broadcast on the MSU radio station for all Muslims to join the rebels and overthrow the administration of President Marcos. On the following day, when military reinforcements arrived, the rebels fled to the hills behind the campus.

The Moro National Liberation Front (MNLF) was founded in 1968 under the chairmanship of Nur Misuari, a former economics professor at the University of the Philippines. Abhood Syed Lingga, Chairman of the Political Section of the MNLF in northern Mindanao, in an interview in October 1975, said that the MNLF grew out of Muslim student activity in Manila in the 1960s and was expedited by the "Jabidah (Corregidor) Massacre." He concludes, "MNLF was conceived at the University of the Philippines, Plaza Miranda, and Mindanao State University." It came out in the open after martial law was proclaimed in September 1972 (Linga, 1975: 1). The MNLF military arm is the Bangsa Moro Army (BMA), which had the goal of establishing a separate nation known as Bangsa Moro. The BMA received support and training from Libya and Malaysia (Ayoob, 1981: 219; McAmis, 1973: 10-13).

The conflict continued to spread from Cotabato to Lanao to Zamboanga, then to the Sulu Archipelago. On February 6, 1974, there was a major battle in the town of Jolo, Sulu, between the MNLF and the armed forces of the Philippines (AFP). The town was heavily damaged from offshore bombardment by the Philippine navy. Losses on both sides were heavy: hundreds of soldiers, civilians, and rebels killed. The battle was followed by much looting. Saudi Arabia offered to help in the rebuilding of Jolo (Majul, 1985: 65). Another Muslim Manifesto issued in April 1974 called for the withdrawal of all government troops, the return of all land taken from the Moros, and the implementation of Islamic law (shariah) and customs in all Muslim areas. The GRP answer was to send in more troops until about 75 percent of the AFP were assigned to deal with the Muslim rebellion.

The MNLF not only gained material support from other Muslim

countries, but also won diplomatic recognition from the Organization of the Islamic Conference (OIC). The OIC convinced the MNLF to drop its demands for secession and to seek meaningful autonomy for the Muslims in the southern Philippines. In 1975 the OIC requested the GRP to accept the inseparable unity of the Bangsa Moro people and their homeland in Mindanao. The fighting continued during these negotiations.

The MNLF considered itself a movement for social reform in the entire Muslim Filipino community. They had no respect for the older, traditional Muslim leaders whom they considered as pawns of the majority Christian government. The Bangsa Moro Army was estimated to vary in manpower from 5,000 to 30,000 armed troops divided in different commands in different Muslim ethnic groups (Ferrer, 1997: 215).

With internal pressures from the church and external pressures from Muslim countries, including the threat to cut off oil shipments from Saudi Arabia (Iran stopped sending oil to the Philippines), the Marcos Martial Law government negotiated the "Tripoli Agreement" with the assistance of Imelda Marcos and President Muammar al-Qadhdhafi of Libya and four representatives of the Organization of the Islamic Conference (OIC). This Tripoli Agreement called for a ceasefire in December 1976, with terms of a peace agreement still to be finalized. This would allow for autonomy in thirteen provinces with Muslim courts and security forces. The Islamic Conference of Foreign Ministers (ICFM) blamed the GRP for breaking the Tripoli Agreement (Ayoob, 1981: 225).

The MNLF began to break up as Misuari spent his time between Libya and Iran. Hashim Salamat, a Maguindanaon based in Cairo and Pakistan, left the MNLF Central Committee and formed the Moro Islamic Liberation Front (MILF). Salamat had been trained in Malaysia and wished to have a firm Islamic policy compared to Misuari's alleged Marxist leanings. The MILF was reported to have 14,280 members in 1993, mostly from Cotabato and Lanao (Ferrer, 1997: 215). Dimas Pundato was an MNLF vice-chairman from the Maranao Muslims of Lanao del Sur. In March 1982, he broke with Misuari and formed the MNLF-Reformist Group (RF). This group was headed by Maranao elite. The MNLF-RF aimed to establish an Islamic society within a Moro province under shariah by negotiations with the GRP (Ferrer, 1997: 216).

Former members of MNLF also established a militant Muslim group called Mujahedeen Commando Freedom Fighters (also known as Abu Sayyaf). This fundamentalist or extremist group has operated in Zamboanga and Basilan through terrorist activities of bombings and kidnappings in the late 1980s and 1990s (Ferrer, 1997).

The divisions in the Filipino Muslim political groups are mainly along ethnic or tribal lines. This demonstrates a major weakness of the Muslim minority in negotiating with the GRP for Muslim concerns. There are several other Muslim groups all claiming to represent all Muslim Filipinos.

After the Tripoli Agreement, the MNLF seemed to lose much of its momentum and intensity. This may have been due to reduced support from other Muslim sources. Another reason was an increased concern for Muslim Filipinos shown by various activities of the GRP. As a result of offering amnesty to former MNLF troops, large numbers surrendered to the government. The GRP made concessions to satisfy Muslim concerns by establishing the Muslim Amanah Bank. It also arranged to implement a Muslim Personal Law Code. Islamic schools received government recognition and support; Islamic holidays were proclaimed in Muslim areas. The year 1980 marked the beginning of 1400 A.H. — the beginning of the fifteenth century of Islam. It also marked the 600th anniversary of the arrival of Islam in the Philippine island of Sulu in 1380 A.D. For the first time the GRP called attention to these Muslim anniversaries. President and Mrs. Marcos also inaugurated the Muslim village Maharlika in Metro Manila. A new mosque was built with government funds in downtown Manila. Despite isolated violent acts, the pace of fighting decreased in the 1980s. The Philippine government and society had begun to recognize that Muslim Filipinos were citizens as much as Christian Filipinos even though Muslims represented a small percentage of the total population — around 4.5 percent at most (McAmis, 1983: 35, 36). Muslim sources continue to quote a much higher percentage — from 8 to 12 percent — but a careful, objective, historical analysis of reliable Philippine statistics from 1918 to 1998 reveals the most accurate, reliable percentage is less than 4.5 percent (Gowing, 1979[b]: 254) living in western Mindanao and the Sulu Archipelago.

One other factor that should be mentioned is the concern Christian church leaders had for the welfare of Muslim Filipinos. As the level of fighting increased, the National Council of Churches in the Philippines (NCCP) formed a Muslim-Christian Reconciliation Study Committee (MCRSC) to promote understanding between Muslims and Christians and to seek nonviolent solutions to some of the problems in the southern Philippines. This committee was composed of representatives of various Protestant churches and the Roman Catholic Church with Muslims invited as advisors. One result was the promotion of Muslim-Christian dialogue at the local, national, and international levels. Another result was the beginning of a "Program Aimed at Christian Education About Muslims" (PACEM) for local churches. This helped in a small way to improve understanding and acceptance between Muslims and Christians. It is impossible to measure the full impact of such efforts on changing the attitudes and removing centuries-old prejudice, but a beginning has been made that can produce positive results in the future. The Islamic resurgence in the southern Philippines has resulted in various churches talking and planning together on how to improve relations between Muslims and Christians (McAmis, 1983: 33, 34).

It is evident from the Philippine experience that it is not possible to solve ethnic-religious problems through socio-economic programs or through military action. If national self-determination is considered a fundamental human right, then serious thought and joint action must be considered and implemented to satisfy the special concerns and needs of the minority Muslim Filipinos.

"If at first you don't succeed, try, try again!" This seems to have been the motto of Nur Misuari as he continued diplomatic efforts for Bangsamoro autonomy in the Philippines and abroad. His main Muslim channels continued to be the Organization of the Islamic Conference (OIC) and the Islamic Foreign Minister Conference (IFMC).[16] A meeting of the IFMC in Kuala Lumpur, Malaysia, called for a "just solution to the Mindanao Problem." The Indonesian delegate insisted on adding the phrase "within the framework of the national sovereignty and territorial integrity of the Philippines." Malaysia, in spite of earlier tensions over the claim to Sabah, took the same position. Libya proposed to condemn the Philippines for oppression of the Moros. Again, Indonesia and Malaysia warned about interfering in the internal affairs of the Philippines. Both Malaysia and Indonesia have been encouraging a peaceful solution to the Mindanao problem, not only for ASEAN unity, but also to prevent the Philippine situation from influencing their own delicate communal problems. Both Indonesia and Malaysia have assured the GRP that they discourage their citizens from giving assistance to Moro rebels. In this matter there was harmony among these three Malay nations of Southeast Asia (Gowing, 1982[a]: 20).

16. IFMC, ICFM, and OIC are interchangeable. OIC is the most widely used by the Western media.

The late former Senator Benigno Aquino conducted unofficial personal diplomacy with Misuari in an effort to reach agreement on Muslim autonomy in the southern Philippines. Aquino had reportedly tried to reconcile the leaders of the various Filipino Muslim factions. In one meeting in Taif, Saudi Arabia, in May 1983, he assumed that there was a "unity pact" between Misuari and Salamat. This was an illusion. Aquino felt that Misuari was the key to solving the Mindanao problem; he did not realize how serious the ethnic and personal differences were among the major groups of Muslim Filipinos.

When the wife of Aquino, Corazon Aquino, became president of the Philippines after the "People's Power" overthrow of President Marcos in February 1986, she took the dramatic step of meeting with Nur Misuari in his Bangsa Moro hometown of Maimbung, Sulu, on September 5, 1986. She showed that she was more than willing to go many extra miles for peace in the southern Philippines. This meeting led to an agreement for a ceasefire with the MNLF and the AFP. It also provided an opportunity to find a solution to the ongoing conflict.

This opened the way for further negotiations in Saudi Arabia that led to the "Jeddah Accords" in January 1987. The MNLF raised the stakes, demanding that twenty-three provinces be included in the autonomous Muslim area. When it was mentioned that this would violate the new 1986 Philippine constitution, the MNLF responded that it did not recognize the Philippine constitution.

In 1987 the Aquino administration formed the Mindanao Regional Consultative Commission (MRCC) to help congress draft an organic act for the proposed autonomous region of Muslim Mindanao (ARMM). The MNLF did not accept the recommendations of the MRCC. The MNLF then tried the tactic of applying for full membership in the OIC as a sovereign state so that they could negotiate with the Philippines on a state-to-state basis. The OIC did not approve the MNLF application (*Waging Peace*, 1989: 178, 179).

The MILF denounced the 1987 Jeddah Accords and declared that only an agreement reached through conflict negotiations on neutral ground under the auspices of OIC and/or the Muslim World League (MWL) could assess the Bangsamoro peoples' rights to self-government. The MILF further declared that it seeks autonomy, not secession. It would disarm after a suitable agreement has been reached (*Waging Peace*, 1989: 200, 201).

Negotiations were continued with the Aquino administration until

1991. A peace commission was established, but no agreements were reached with MNLF or MILF before the Ramos administration began in 1992. The fourth round of formal peace talks between the GRP and MNLF was held in Indonesia on August 30, 1996. The "Final Agreement on the implementation of the 1976 Tripoli Agreement between the Government of the Republic of the Philippines (GRP) and the Moro National Liberation Front (MNLF) with the participation of the Organization of the Islamic Conference Ministerial Committee of Six and the Secretary General of the Organization of the Islamic Conference" was finally reached after twenty years of intermittent negotiations between the GRP and MNLF (Ferrer, 1997: 198). The agreement was signed by President Ramos and Misuari on September 2, 1996, in Malacanang Palace in Manila. This agreement provides an Autonomous Region for Muslim Mindanao (ARMM) in fourteen provinces (thirteen plus the newly created province of Saranggani) and nine cities created by the 1996 Peace Agreement under Presidential Executive Order. This included the creation of a special Zone of Peace and Development (ZOPAD) under the Southern Philippines Council for Peace and Development (SPCPD), which shall exist for a period of three years to implement intensive programs for peace and development. During this three-year period, Congress is to amend or repeal the Organic Act creating the ARMM (RA6734). The new law shall then be submitted to a referendum in the provinces and cities concerned. Other provisions of this agreement call for MNLF troops to be integrated into the Philippine National Police (PNP) and the Armed Forces of the Philippines (AFP). Elections were held on September 9, 1996, and MNLF Chairman Professor Nur Misuari was elected as chairman of ARMM and the SPCPD without any opposition (Ferrer, 1997: 199-200).

At the close of 1999, the three-year trial period is almost finished. Many MNLF members who did not accept this agreement have joined the MILF and Abu Sayyaf. The level of violence has been reduced considerably. Efforts for development in ZOPAD/ARMM have received financial assistance from the GRP and several foreign donors, including USAID. The results are not clear at this time — some claim funds were not released while others say funds were not used for projects. The GRP is still negotiating with MILF, which insists on a stronger Islamic emphasis in the ARMM. This is difficult to implement with a 77 percent Christian majority in the fourteen provinces and nine cities. Only four of the provinces have a Muslim majority, and these four were the only ones who voted to be included in the previous Autonomous Region of Muslim Mindanao. These four provinces are still "high risk" areas where it is not safe for unescorted aid workers and outside visitors to go to assess the present unstable situation. At the end of 1999, there is still no satisfactory, permanent answer to the "Mindanao Problem" or the "Muslim Problem" or the "Moro Problem." In August, 1999, a "Mindanao Peace Forum" was held at the University of the Philippines to evaluate the results of AARM, ZOPAD, and SPCPD. Muslim and government representatives could not agree on any permanent, positive results of this three-year period or make realistic recommendations for the continuation of these projects to promote peace.

At the time of this writing in September, 1999, the Congress of the Philippines has proposed delaying elections in the ARMM and SPCPD from September 1999 to March 2000. The Senate has not yet acted and must still revise the Organic Act for possible expansion of ARMM to be submitted to voters in the area as a referendum. There seems to be no realistic possibility that the nine provinces with a large Christian majority would approve their inclusion in an Autonomous Region of Muslim Mindanao (ARMM). The four provinces with a Muslim majority are divided among four Muslim ethnic groups — Maguindanao, Maranao, Taosug, and Samal — with no historic unity.

Muslim Filipinos have made many gains in basic human rights in the past forty years. They are free to practice and spread the Muslim faith in all parts of the Philippines. Islamic resurgence has led to a more faithful practice and teaching of classical "high Islam." There are a growing number of converts to Islam from the Roman Catholic Church. Certainly there are many more converts to Islam from the church than from Islam to Christianity. A Christian Filipino church leader reports that several priests from both the Roman Catholic and the Philippine Independent Catholic Church have become Muslims. Muslim Filipinos have an aggressive da'wa mission in the traditional Christian areas of Mindanao, Metro Manila, and other cities. They are free to hold rallies, use the media, and build mosques everywhere. Christian missionary efforts are prohibited or severely restricted in Muslim areas (Gomez, 1977: 20). In July 1999 there were newspaper reports of a Christian evangelistic campaign in Basilan where hand grenades were exploded in the crowd during the revival. The Abu Sayyaf was suspected of this and other violent acts including continued kidnapping of foreign development workers.

The GRP has refused to consider granting secession or independence to Muslim citizens living in the southern Philippines. Muslims have decreased their demands from secession to autonomy, and have reduced the area for autonomy from the entire island of Mindanao and Sulu to twenty-three provinces, and finally to fourteen provinces and nine cities. Yet the Muslims represent only 23 percent of the population in ZOPAD. This means that if there is going to be true peace and development, Muslims and Christians residing in these fourteen provinces and nine cities must realistically face the situation as it is if they are to live together, plan together, and work together for the benefit of both communities in Western Mindanao and Sulu. Centuries of fighting, prejudice, and rejection cannot be overcome in a few years. There has been much improvement in relationships in the last forty years. In the closing chapter, we will consider several possibilities for Malays in Southeast Asia to improve understanding, relationships, and society for the benefit of all. In this way Muslims and Christians can become true friends and another Qur'anic verse can serve as an inspiration to both groups:

> "You will find your best friends among those
> who call themselves Christians."

6 · The Role of the Church and Islam in Malay Southeast Asia in the Twenty-First Century

According to reliable population estimates for the year 2000 A.D./1420 A.H., Christians and Muslims comprise just over half of the entire world's people. Christians outnumber Muslims on the ratio of around two-to-one. In Malay Southeast Asia, including Indonesia, Malaysia, and the Philippines, the total population is estimated to be 310,470,000 people. Christians and Muslims represent 94 percent of this total. Here the Muslims outnumber the Christians two-to-one. Most of the Muslims are in Indonesia (186,322,000), while the majority of Christians are found in the Philippines (67,500,000). Malaysia has just over 50 percent Muslims; 98 percent of them are Malays (13,730,000). This leaves only 6 percent of the population represented by other minority religious and ethnic groups — Hindus, Buddhists, Confucianists, Sikhs, and animistic tribal religions. Therefore, our focus in this concluding chapter will be on the role of Malay Christians and Muslims in the future developments in Malay Southeast Asia. The future role and status of the small minority groups need to be remembered also.

A. Prospects for Christian-Muslim Relations Among the Malays

After more than 500 years of conflict, confrontation, and competition between Islam and the Western Church in Malay Southeast Asia, what are the

103

possibilities for the indigenous Malay population of 65 percent Muslim and 29 percent Christian to work together in peaceful cooperation and development in the next millennium? What contribution can I, a retired Western Lutheran missionary who has spent forty-four years in Southeast Asia, make in providing useful answers and suggestions to this question? I want to share what I have learned from both Muslim and Christian Malay friends and from my experience in promoting and encouraging positive, improved Christian-Muslim relationships in the southern Philippines for the past thirty-seven years. I may not be here to observe what happens in the new millennium, but my hope and prayer is that my past efforts will make a small contribution toward friendly relationships, trust, and cooperation of all Malay Muslims and Christians. It has been my experience that a good Muslim and a good Christian make good friends and neighbors.

Many economists have predicted that the twenty-first century will be "the Asian Century" with the People's Republic of China playing a major role. If Malay Christians and Muslims work together, the possibilities for growth and development are unlimited. Great advances can soon be realized in much-needed improvements in health, education, agriculture, housing, social welfare, modern communication, and transportation. Two major health problems are common: high infant mortality rates and shorter lifespan than found in more developed areas. Surely it is God's will that the 94 percent Muslim-Christian Malay population work together to improve the lifestyle and lifespan of all people living in the tropical islands of Southeast Asia. In the first half of the 1990s, it appeared that Asia was on its way with rapid, sustained economic growth, especially in Southeast Asia. Then the "economic crisis" or "economic meltdown" hit Southeast Asia with a vengeance and drastically reduced the internal and external economic developments. In 1999 this area is slowly recovering from this severe setback. The political and economic situation is more stable, and minimal growth has resumed.

If Malay Southeast Asia is to again participate in the "economic miracle" of the "Asian Century," full cooperation, understanding, and involvement of Indonesia, Malaysia, and the Philippines will be necessary. A prerequisite for this mutual development is to have positive relationships between Muslims and Christians on the national and regional level among all Malays. This requires diplomacy — which is described as the art of the possible — at all levels in these three nations.

These three nations, because of the Malay population, have much more in common than other nations of Southeast Asia or the whole of Asia. In the 1960s a political-economic organization called MAPHILINDO (Malaysia-Philippines-Indonesia) was formed to plan and implement development proposals. This organization evolved into the Association of Southeast Asian Nations (ASEAN) with two additional members — Thailand and Brunei. Proposals remained in the planning stage and closer ties were realized. Now ASEAN has expanded to include Singapore, Vietnam, Laos, and Cambodia with the renegade nation of Myanmar (formerly Burma) being offered membership along with East Timor, if it becomes independent. At a meeting of ASEAN in July 1999, in Singapore, the United States, the European Union, and China were invited as guests. ASEAN has a tremendous economic and political potential. The Malay countries have a leading role to play in promoting peace and economic development throughout Southeast Asia. In 1980 one observer wrote that the most serious threat to unity and continuity of ASEAN was the Philippines because of the conflict between Muslims and Christians in the southern Philippines. This centuries-old conflict received new energy and support from Islamic resurgence. This demonstrates the importance of positive, stable relationships in Southeast Asia if economic and social development are to become a reality (Trocki, 1980: 153).

In referring to the five original members of ASEAN, one scholar wrote on the topic, "Islam: Threat to ASEAN." His main emphasis was on the role of Islam in Indonesia, Malaysia, and the Philippines:

> Currently, all the ASEAN governments continue to hold the balance of power in their respective states. In each case, however, Islam presents a new area of increasing tension, both internally and externally. (Trocki, 1980: 149)

He points out that faithful Muslims are not satisfied with the secular political and social order. "Because of this, Islam may be seen as a potential threat to the stability of the ASEAN alliance." In Indonesia the secularization of nationalism was built on the Dutch colonial policy and other Western models. The Malay Muslims of Malaysia are more faithful in their Islamic practice than most of the Malay Muslims of Indonesia. Malaysia is a key member of ASEAN. An internal shift in Malaysia's social balance could threaten the unity of ASEAN if the tension increases between ethnic concerns and nationalism (Trocki, 1980: 152).

Secularism in modern government and economics is a real threat to both Islam and the church because it does not recognize that there is a God or that God is sovereign in every area of life. Thus, both Christians and Muslims can emphasize in their respective communities the role of faith in God and his guidance in the lives of all people and nations. This is one area where positive Christian-Muslim relations can show the dangers of secularism and materialism in the world today. We will explore how the church and Islam can work together in other areas that may be divisive and confrontational.

B. Christian Mission and Islamic Da'wa

We have learned that the most common characteristic of the global Islamic resurgence is the emphasis on and the practice of *da'wa (da'wah* or *dak'wah).* Da'wa is the obedience to the mandate "to call men into the path of Allah" (Qur'an 16:25). Faithful Muslims who are committed to da'wa believe it is their duty to share the teachings of Islam with all other humans. Da'wa is directed internally to those who are already Muslims and directed externally to all those who are not Muslims to invite and encourage them to become Muslims by completely submitting themselves to the will of God according to the Qur'an and Sunnah. To become a Muslim, a person must testify in Arabic and with sincere intention, "There is no God but God, and Muhammad is the Apostle of God." Da'wa is an invitation to accept Islam as a way of faith and a way of life. Da'wa is directed to everyone to become a member of the *ummah,* the worldwide community of all Muslims.

The Christian Mission is the mandate given to all members of the church to go into all the world and preach the gospel (good news) to all people. Jesus Christ issued this "Great Commission" to the early church: "All authority has been given to me in heaven and on earth. Go, therefore, and make disciples of all nations, teaching them all things that I have commanded you and baptizing them in the name of the Father and of the Son and of the Holy Spirit." Every faithful Christian knows that it is his/her personal responsibility and privilege to share his/her faith in Jesus the Christ as Lord and Savior. Every Christian is to witness by word and deed what Christ means to him/her. Every Christian commits his/her entire life to God in Holy Baptism to do the will of God and to forsake the devil and his evil ways. Every Christian can say with confidence, "I live, yet not I, but Christ lives in me and the life that I now live in the flesh, I live by faith in the Son of God who loved me and gave himself for me." The motive and message is that each person may know that he is reconciled to God and has the sure promise of forgiveness of sins and eternal life in heaven to join in praising and thanking God. Who is Christ? What has he done for me? How can I receive the benefits of his ministry? These are the questions that the Christian Mission answers.

Both Islam and Christianity, then, are missionary religions. Both Islam and the church have a missionary mandate to proclaim the message from God to the whole world. Both Islam and the church are convinced that the faith they proclaim is inclusive and exclusive. This means that Islam is for all who accept its message, but those who reject it are excluded from the *ummah,* the community of God's people on earth. The church believes that the good news about Jesus the Christ is for all people, and all who believe it are members of the one holy, catholic, apostolic church. Those who reject the good news are not reconciled to God and will be separated from him in eternity. Thus, Christian Mission and Islamic da'wa place Islam and the church not only in competition, but also on a collision course that can lead to competition, confrontation, and conflict. In order to deal with these issues on an intellectual, rational level, the World Council of Churches and the Islamic Foundation sponsored a Dialogue Consultation on "Christian Mission and Islamic Da'wah," on June 26-30, 1976/ Jumada 28–Rajab 4, 1396, in Geneva. This conference was attended by seven Muslim and seven Christian scholars who were recognized authorities in the teachings of Islam and the church. Several position papers on da'wa and mission were presented and freely discussed. The latter part of the consultation concentrated on issues and concerns under the theme "Toward a *Modus Vivendi*" between Christians and Muslims engaged in da'wa and mission. This produced six questions that need to be given priority to promote understanding and acceptance between those engaged in da'wa and mission:

1. By what criteria can we distinguish legitimate mission and da'wah activity?
2. What are the requirements and limitations of religious freedom?
3. How do we encourage mutual respect for legitimate activities of mission and da'wah?

4. By what practical methods can we make effective our repudiation of what we see to be illegitimate activities of mission and da'wah?
5. How can Christians and Muslims cooperate in what is an imperative of their respective faiths, that is, to serve their fellow man in need?
6. What recommendations do we wish to make regarding future studies, dialogue, and other activities? (*Christian Mission and Islamic Da'wah,* 1981: 95)

These questions form the basis for a fruitful discussion between any group of rational, informed Christians and Muslims of goodwill. This consultation on Mission and da'wa did not provide complete answers to all the six questions, but it did issue a "Statement" that provides guidelines and possibilities on how both Muslims and Christians in Malay Southeast Asia can fulfill the mandate for Mission and da'wa in a peaceful manner.

One significant statement reads, "The conference upholds the principle of religious freedom recognizing that the Muslims, as well as the Christian, must enjoy the full liberty *to convince or be convinced* (emphasis mine) and to practice their faith and order their religious life in accordance with their own religious laws and principles" (*Christian Mission and Islamic Da'wah,* 1981: 100).

Another agreed statement:

The conference was grieved to hear that some Christians in some Muslim countries have felt themselves limited in the exercise of their religious freedom and have been denied the right to church buildings. The Muslim participants regard such violation as contrary to Islamic law as well as the principle of religious freedom enunciated above. (*Christian Mission and Islamic Da'wah,* 1982: 100)

The Christians expressed their deep regret and sympathy for all the moral wrongs against Muslims perpetrated by Christians during the colonial period. This resulted in Muslims and Christians in these countries being estranged from each other instead of cooperating for the common good. They confessed that many Western missionaries cooperated with these colonial powers and contributed to the inhumane abuses. Now that the period of colonialism has ended and a new relationship is desirable between Christians and Muslims, most Muslims are still suspicious of Christian missionaries and their motives.

The conference was aware of the dire need for reciprocal understanding of history, theology, moral and legal teachings, social and political theories, and problems of acculturation and modernization faced by the two faiths. This requires serious study and research. They urged the Vatican, World Council of Churches, and international Islamic organizations to sponsor conferences on these subjects (*Christian Mission and Islamic Da'wah*, 1981: 101).

The full proceedings of this Chambesy Dialogue Consultation were published by both the *International Review of Missions* and the *Islamic Foundation*. The discussions and recommendations of this landmark consultation could help to avoid misunderstanding and conflict between Malay Christians and Muslims in Southeast Asia if they were translated, distributed, and heeded by all those engaged in mission and da'wa in this part of the world. Mutual understanding and cooperation is necessary if Malays are going to witness development and economic growth to remove poverty, injustice, and oppression among all Malays in the twenty-first century.

An Asian Christian leader has said that the church must have an understanding of Malay Islam not based on research by Western Christian scholars but on the writings of Malay Muslims. He adds that Muslims and Christians must cooperate in promoting social justice as long as it is not in a nation state based on Islam. All Malaysian groups must participate in creating a just society based on equal rights. Islam or the church cannot dictate the political policies of the government. There must be mutual agreement on economic and legal principles so that all faiths can work together for a society that respects the rights of all. He reminds the minorities that the Islamic *ummah* excludes other faiths and does not prescribe equal rights for all members of society (Yap, 1980: 43, 44).

He further advises Christians to understand Islamic revival as an effort to be more spiritual. He encourages Christians to strengthen their commitments to Christ through more Bible study and following the example of the life of Christ. There must be more Muslim-Christian cooperation in living together at the local village level (Yap, 1980: 43, 44).

When I think of sharing my faith in Christ with my Muslim neighbor, I can never forget what my Maranao neighbor, a young lawyer and a practicing, faithful, knowledgeable Muslim, said to me: "If you do not share your faith with me and tell me what is nearest and dearest to your heart and life — your faith in Christ — I will consider it an insult." This was an invitation to witness to him about what Christ means to me. I certainly did not wish to insult my Muslim neighbor. If only all Muslims and Christians would have this feeling and attitude! Christian mission and Islamic da'wa are nothing more and nothing less than sharing with our neighbor that which is nearest and dearest to our heart and life. Can this not best be done in a loving, friendly, reciprocal manner? That brings us to another way of improving Christian-Muslim relations through interreligious dialogue — another way to share faith and life in a peaceful manner.

C. Christian-Muslim Dialogue Among the Malays

1. Dialogue in General

After World War II, the "Ecumenical Movement" became increasingly active among most Protestant and Orthodox churches. This led to the formation of the World Council of Churches (WCC), which included most of the Baptist, Anglican, Lutheran, Orthodox, Reformed, and Evangelical communities in an effort to promote cooperation and seek church unity. The Ecumenical Movement led to a series of serious discussions or dialogues between various denominations; that is, Lutheran-Reformed, Anglican-Lutheran, Reformed-Orthodox. The Roman Catholic Church was also involved in dialogue with Lutherans, Reformed, Anglican, Orthodox, and other churches. Vatican II, held in the early 1960s, led to the Roman Catholic Church to more dialogue and involvement with other Christian communions.

This intra-Christian dialogue was soon expanded to include other faiths. The WCC formed a division known as the Sub-unit for Dialogue with People of Living Faiths and Ideologies (DFI). The DFI and the Vatican sponsored Jewish-Christian dialogue, Muslim-Christian dialogue, Buddhist-Christian dialogue, Christian-Communist dialogue, etc. Dialogue became a popular and effective instrument for understanding people with different faiths and ideologies. This spread to many parts of the world. Dialogues have been held in Geneva, Rome, Spain, and the U.S. Muslim countries have sponsored Muslim-Christian Dialogue in Lebanon, Egypt, Tunisia, and Libya (McAmis, 1987: 18-21). A dialogue was held on November 6-7, 1998, at Washington, D.C., under the sponsorship of the Episcopal Commission of Ecumenical and Interreligious Ministries and the Royal Embassy of Saudi Arabia. The theme of the dialogue was, "The Two Sacred Paths: Christianity and Islam — a Call for Understanding" (*Cantilevers*, 1999: 64).

Dr. Peter Gowing, a Christian scholar respected by Muslim Filipinos, informed us that in the history of Southeast Asia there have been three basic types of relationships between Malay Muslims and Christians. The first was "Crusade" or "Confrontation," which began with the arrival of the Portuguese Christians in Malacca in 1511. The "Crusade" mentality against the Moros was continued by Spain in the Philippines. This attitude has continued in various forms up to the present time.

The second type of relationship is "Apartheid" or "Separation," which means that Muslims and Christians live in separate areas and go their separate ways. They have as little contact as possible in social, political, educational, and economic activities. This continues in the "leave us alone" attitude of the Malays in Malaysia and in many parts of the Philippines.

The third type of relationship is "Dialogue," which promotes communication and understanding between Christians and Muslims. Through meaningful, serious dialogue, Muslims and Christians begin to trust and accept one another as fellow human beings. They learn how to live and work together in peace and friendship while sharing many of the same hopes and fears regarding the future.

Dialogue then can serve as a valuable means of promoting peace and development among the Malays of Southeast Asia. We will now examine the question "What is dialogue?" The essence of dialogue is the meeting between persons (not religious systems) in mutual respect, frankness, and sincerity. Dialogue is listening to the other person so well that you can repeat exactly what that person said to you. Dialogue is speaking from the heart about your faith and life.

Dialogue is two-way communication, including speaking and listening. Dialogue is sharing of innermost thoughts, feelings, beliefs, hopes, and fears. Dialogue is caring for the other participants in dialogue. Dialogue is learning and growing. Dialogue is an attempt to put yourself inside the skin of another person. Dialogue is trying to fully understand the other. Dialogue is a friendly, empathetic exchange between me and thee. Religious dialogue is a sharing of faith with someone of another faith with the awareness that God is present. Dialogue is trust, openness, and honesty in a two-way exchange of views and perceptions.

Dialogue is not debate. Dialogue is not *mission* or *da'wa*. There are no winners or losers, only learners and seekers. Dialogue is not an attempt to convert or convince the other person, not a display of wisdom and intellectual skills. It is not trying to put the other person down. It is not coercive or persuasive. It is not political even when it deals with political concerns. Dialogue is not negotiation.

Perhaps the following theological perspective can help to better understand interreligious dialogue:

> Dialogue starts from the assumptions that each religion has its absolute claim which cannot be relativized. No amount of reformulation will do away with the difference. But, by letting our theologizing be influenced by others, we will be forced to greater honesty and deeper spirituality. The prerequisite for dialogue is not the harmonizing of all beliefs, but the recognition that each spiritual person has a committed and absolute conviction, and that these convictions are different. The Christian is committed to God through Christ; the Muslim to the Qur'an as God's final word; the Hindu to the idea of many paths to the One Brahman (the absolutizing of a relativism), and so on. In the dialogical approach, each religion is seen as having an absolute that cannot be surrendered without destroying the essential identity of that faith. Such dialogue necessitates sufficient maturity of the ego "to let the opposite co-exist without pretending that they can be made compatible." Indeed the very capacity and need for categorical assertion is understood as held in common by all religious persons, and as such is a ground for dialogue. (Coward, 1985: 39)

The purpose of dialogue is to promote understanding between two or more persons or groups where before there was misunderstanding. Dialogue is to provide opportunity for each participant to share fears, doubts, concerns, sorrows, joys, hopes, and dreams. The purpose of dialogue is to learn to live together in peace and love with all other people. It is to strengthen bonds with our fellow human beings and to recognize that, in spite of our many differences, we all share the risks and dangers, together with all the opportunities and resources, that life on this planet offers.

Formal dialogue is the usual type of dialogue meant when we talk about religious dialogue. It means that a definite time and place have been agreed upon. Often a basic theme has been approved to guide the discussion toward a certain topic or problem. There can be no attempt to control or guide the direction of the dialogue; that is up to the participants. Sometimes it has been helpful in larger groups to divide into smaller groups of no more than ten persons for part of the discussion, and then have a plenary session to present and discuss the summary and findings of the smaller groups.

It has also been learned that a live-in dialogue has a better opportunity to give the participants more time to get better acquainted and to fully discuss all issues inside and outside of scheduled sessions. A live-in dialogue means that all participants are housed in the same facility and eat together in a common dining area. Live-in dialogues are usually scheduled for a minimum of two days.

Informal dialogue is a "dialogue in life" where Muslims and Christians live together as neighbors and work together in various jobs or attend school together. Informal dialogue provides an opportunity to share one's faith and concerns with someone of another faith. These are not scheduled encounters but natural opportunities for dialogue in daily life situations. This type of dialogue can be useful in removing misunderstanding and prejudices.

Whether formal or informal, the ongoing nature of dialogue needs to be stressed. In a formal dialogue the participants often arrive at a large degree of mutual understanding, and close friendships are formed after several days together. However, when the dialogue is over and the participants return to their respective homes and occupations, often the dialogue remains as nothing more than a pleasant afterglow. What is needed is to encourage each participant to continue in a formal and informal way to share experiences of the dialogue with friends, neighbors, and colleagues so that the effects of the dialogue can be multiplied. Also, the results of the dialogue need to be shared in printed form with all those concerned. Sometimes a follow-up dialogue is needed to see that the matters agreed upon are presented to those who can act upon them. It can also be helpful to hold a second or third dialogue with the same participants after an interval of time to carry the discussion to a higher level.

For lack of a better term, dialogue-in-print refers to a scholarly dialogue in published reports, articles, books, and journals. In this way dialogue can be possible without necessarily gathering the participants in one place. Such types of dialogue-in-print can be widely circulated with responses made in a spirit of friendship and reconciliation, in a sincere effort to promote intellectual growth and cross-fertilization of thoughts.

2. *Muslim-Christian Dialogue in Indonesia*

At the end of the twentieth century, Indonesia is faced with political, economic, religious, and international problems. A new generation of leaders will lead Indonesia into the twenty-first century. They will not have the stature and military support of Sukarno and Suharto, who led Indonesia since independence from 1945 to 1998. A new consensus will have to be found among the more than 214 million citizens. The population has seen drastic changes in education and religion. In contrast to what was reported earlier, the santri are increasing in number and influence. Many santri are promoting the Islamization of the government.

Clifford Geertz, who wrote *The Religion of Java* in 1960, returned to Indonesia after thirty years and discovered that the younger generation of *abangan* are becoming *santri* at a rapid rate. This means that devout, practicing Muslims will be the majority in the twenty-first century. Even the rural areas have experienced increasing Islamization under the Suharto administration (Tamara, 1986: 27, 28). In the future the government will offer more opportunities for faithful Muslims in the military and various departments. The *ulama* are afraid of "militant Islam" as seen in Acheh, with their frequent demands for autonomy or secession. This leads the *ulama* to closer cooperation with the government.

Is Indonesia headed for an Islamic state or an Islamic democracy in the new century? Muslim influence in politics will continue to grow. Muslim leaders will need the guidance of experienced, respected political and economic advisors in order to enjoy a prosperous, stable democracy that avoids the extremes of militant fundamentalism and the pitfalls of communist socialism, which almost gained control of Indonesia near the end of the long period under President Sukarno. Here is where the positive influence of Indonesia's Christian minority groups can help to establish smooth working relationships internally and externally with the West (Tamara, 1986: 29).

Indonesians have a long-standing formula for solving community problems. In Bahasa Indonesia it is called *mushawara-mufakat,* which means discussion/consensus. *Mushawara* continues in the group's discussing of any community problem until consensus, *mufakat,* is reached. I have seen this method at work in the Maranao area of the southern Philippines, and it really works. This method of conflict or dispute resolution is a Malay custom of long standing. It works much better than the democratic method of voting — the majority wins and the minority loses. In mushawara/ mufakat, everyone is a winner; there are no losers. Mushawara/mufakat then is the Malay equivalent of dialogue!

Muslims and Christians in Indonesia have worked together to promote religious peace and harmony through dialogue. The Department of Religion has sponsored Muslim-Christian dialogue on the local, regional, national, and international levels. This is an encouraging sign that offers positive results for the twenty-first century. Dialogue concerns not only Muslims and Christians, but also all ethnic and religious groups in majority-minority situations. Dialogue also involves the government in dialogue with delicate religious and cultural concerns.

In 1969 the Indonesian government established a five-year dialogue program with people of different religions. The Department of Religion has organized and sponsored these dialogues up to the present time. Muslim and Christian leaders from various parts of Indonesia have been brought together for several days to exchange viewpoints and concerns. This government-sponsored dialogue is effective in promoting understanding and peaceful relationships between Muslims and Christians in Indonesia (Fitzgerald, 1976: 178-83).

3. Christian-Muslim Dialogue in Malaysia

As previously mentioned, the Islamic resurgence in Malaysia has not only revived Malay Muslims' interest in the spiritual aspects of Islam, it has also resulted in a new interest in religion and culture among the minority religious and ethnic communities in Malaysia. This religious resurgence among Malays and non-Malays can lead to a negative or a positive result. Negative conflict/violence/separation will follow if communal groups decide to exploit their own political, economic, and cultural interests (*Aliran*, 1981: 192-200).

> If, on the other hand, rational, tolerant elements among Malays and non-Malays hold sway, they will be able to harness the religious resurgence toward positive ends. (*Aliran*, 1981: 201)

This positive attitude could lead to interreligious dialogue in Malaysia. Such dialogue would lead to greater trust, understanding, and confidence-building among Malay Muslims and other religious minorities. Such dialogues have already begun on a small scale among Buddhists, Hindus, Christians, and Muslims in Malaysia (*Aliran*, 1981: 201).

In Malaysia, Muslims and Christians and people of other faiths have done joint study to learn what they can do together in planning welfare projects. In 1973 the government sponsored a national seminar to help Muslims, Christians, and other religious minorities plan projects to benefit all needy people. In the same year the government sponsored another national seminar "to see how best Muslim, Christian, Buddhist, Hindu, and other voluntary organizations . . . could maximize their efforts in nation-building in the face of changing values and structure in Malaysia" (*Christians Meeting Muslims*, 1977: 124).

Even more encouraging, the Malaysian Inter-Religious Organization, registered with the government, had the following objectives:

a. to promote peace in Malaysia in particular and the world in general;
b. to practice and spread the idea of the dignity of man and the spirit of brotherhood among all people by transcending the differences of race, nationality, sex, language, and creed;
c. to practice and promote mutual understanding and cooperation among all religions (*Christians Meeting Muslims*, 1977: 124).

Future understanding and trust through interreligious dialogue in Malaysia depend upon the Malay Muslims and the government. The Malay Muslim request to "leave us alone" is opposed to dialogue and can only result in greater misunderstanding and division in Malaysia's future. Also, the general interpretation among Malay Muslims of the Qur'an's verse (2:256), "There shall be no compulsion in religion," is that a non-Muslim can decide to become a Muslim, but a Muslim cannot leave Islam to become a Christian or else he ceases to be a Malay. This indicates a one-way street.

This insecure interpretation of the Quranic verse is refuted by respected Muslim scholars, as we saw in the section on da'wa. Every person has the God-given right, according to Islamic principles, *to convince or be convinced* in matters of religious faith and life (*Christian Mission and Islamic Da'wah*, 1982: 93). This means that a Christian must be open to the possibility that God will lead him to become a Muslim, just as a Muslim must be open to the possibility that God will lead him to become a Christian. Or, as Bishop Kenneth Cragg has affirmed, "A faith you are not free to leave becomes a prison, and no self-respecting faith should be a prison for those within it." Dr. Isma'el al-Faruqi responded, "Islamic law *does* allow a person to exit from the Islamic state" (*Christian Mission and Islamic Da'wah*, 1982: 92).

In this present status of Muslim-Christian relationships in Malaysia, there is very little hope for a sincere dialogue to happen with a 52 percent Malay Muslim majority and a 7 percent Christian minority composed of several non-Malay ethnic groups. Perhaps it would be possible for Malaysian Muslims and Christian participants to be involved in a Second Southeast Asian Muslim-Christian Dialogue as a follow-up to the first dialogue for this region held in Hong Kong in January 1975. The only other slight possibility for Muslim-Christian dialogue in Malaysia would be an informal dialogue-in-life, where Muslims and Christians live as neighbors or as fellow workers or as fellow students. The dialogue-in-print could also promote understanding if Muslims and Christians could read material in Bahasa Malay prepared by respected scholars of each community to learn more about each other's religion.

4. Christian-Muslim Dialogue in the Philippines

As I have been personally involved in Muslim-Christian dialogue in the Philippines as an organizer, facilitator, and participant from 1962 until the present, I must restrain myself and avoid too many personal references in this section. I could easily write a book on this subject alone, but will try to cover only the main issues.

In 1962 the government of the Republic of the Philippines (GRP) held a dialogue of the "Ecumenical Union of Moral Leaders" in Manila. This dialogue included Muslims and Christians. A follow-up dialogue was revived in 1975 by General Fidel V. Ramos. Also in 1975 the GRP held dialogue with Muslim "dissidents" in Zamboanga City to explore an end to conflict and to restore peace and order in the southern Philippines.

Beginning in 1968, Peter Gowing and I planned and held a series of "Annual Seminars on Islam in the Philippines and Asia" (ASIPA). The first seminar had as its theme "Understanding Islam Today," with Roman Catholics and Protestants in attendance at Dansalan College in Marawi City. The second seminar in 1969 was a beginning of a dialogue between Christians and Muslims. These seminar/dialogues continued every year until 1975. As the fighting and tensions increased, in 1972 the name was changed to "Annual Seminar on Mindanao and Sulu Culture" to include concerns of all minorities in the southern Philippines.

The World Council of Churches (WCC) became aware of the involvement of the National Council of Churches in the Philippines (NCCP is a member of WCC) in forming a Muslim-Christian Reconciliation Committee (I chaired MCRC for its three-year period), which introduced a Program Aimed at Christian Education about Muslims (PACEM).

In September 1974, the NCCP, with help of WCC, sponsored the First National Muslim-Christian Dialogue in Zamboanga City under the theme, "Muslims and Christians in Society: Towards Goodwill, Consultation, and Working Together." This was in preparation for the Southeast Asian Muslim-Christian Dialogue with the same theme held in Hong Kong, January 4-10, 1975, with participants from Indonesia, Malaysia, and the Philippines.[1] A Second National Muslim-Christian Dialogue was held

---

1. The Southeast Asian Muslim-Christian Dialogue held in Hong Kong in January, 1975, brought together thirteen Malay Muslims and thirteen Malay Christians from Indonesia, Malaysia, and the Philippines, plus several other Western participants and representatives of the World Council of Churches from Geneva. The governments of all three countries declined to hold this dialogue in their respective nations because it was felt that Muslim-Christian relations were a delicate issue. Thus, Hong Kong was chosen as a neutral setting.

The closing statement of this first Malay Muslim-Christian Dialogue confirms that dialogue can deal with delicate issues and propose practicable solutions. It would be beneficial to reproduce the entire statement, but we have selected a portion of the "Theological basis for Muslim-Christian solutions" and "Building unity in diversity."

We Christians and Muslims meeting in Hong Kong affirm that our respective faiths, properly understood, enjoin on us a loving relationship with each other and with all human beings. The ground and impetus for this loving relationship is no less than the One God Himself who has made all human beings brothers and sisters. Muslims emphasize that God the Compassionate (Al-Rahman) and the Beloved (Al-Habib) commands the faithful to be merciful and compassionate and loving in their dealings with all people, and therefore they are able to be so. The Qur'an embodies this command and specifies ways in which the faithful may obediently comply with it in various life situations. Christians, for their part, emphasize that God's love shown in his self-giving in and through the person of Jesus Christ both inspires and enables their loving relationship with all humankind. Responding to God's love in Jesus Christ, Christians find the example and basis for love in their social dealings with all

at Mindanao State University Campus in January 1976, as conflict between MNLF and AFP was increasing. The Third National Muslim-Christian Dialogue was sponsored by the Muslim community in the Philippines and was held near Manila at Tagaytay City in July 1979. The Fourth National Dialogue was held in Marawi City, November 30 through December 4, 1981, at Dansalan College in Marawi. These dialogues were attended by Muslim and Christian religious, political, and business leaders. All of them made practical recommendations to the government, the business community, and the Christian and Muslim communities to promote peace, development, and justice for all people of the southern Philippines, especially the minorities. The Fifth National Dialogue, in January 1984, was held at Notre Dame of Jolo College and continued to emphasize very practical concerns of the people at the grass roots. The Sixth National Muslim-Christian Dialogue was held in January 1986, at Notre Dame University in Cotabato City with an emphasis from the First Dialogue.

The overall objective of the continuing biennial dialogue is to seek ways and means by which Muslims and Christians can understand each

---

people. Thus allowing for these differences in understanding, both Islam and Christianity find their ethical mandate in the All-Merciful God who loves and is loved.

Because we belong to kindred communities of faith, there are doubtless many things which Christians and Muslims can do together to foster the unity of people in society. Among them we can identify the following:

a. Achieve and maintain peace between themselves since not only national unity but also regional stability are both advanced when the different religious communities live together in peace and harmony.

b. Witness together for the religious and moral perspective that respects the dignity and worth of all human beings in the face of dehumanizing forces.

c. Unite together to strengthen the moral conscience of national endeavor — affirming those aspects of nation-building which operate for the common good — and, in obedience to God's will, calling attention to those aspects which are harmful or oppressive.

d. Promote together a human appreciation of the cultural achievements of all the diverse communities which make up the society — valuing those worthy achievements as the common property of the whole nation and humanity.

e. Represent together the transcendent dimension of human beings in mundane society of men and women, old and young, who in the final analysis belong not only to this world of time and matter but also to the Eternal.

other, cooperate with one another, and work together towards goodwill and consultation. (McAmis, 1987: 66)

The GRP Ministry of Muslim Affairs was the sponsor of the Seventh National Dialogue in December 1987, in Zamboanga City. This was the last of this series of national dialogues, but other formal and informal dialogues continue in the search for peace in the southern Philippines. There have been many measurable and immeasurable benefits from this series of dialogues in the Philippines. If only all the recommendations would be implemented by all Malay Muslims and Malay Christians, there would be a peaceful, prosperous future for all the people of Southeast Asia as we begin the twenty-first century. If only . . . ?!?

In addition to the formal national Muslim-Christian dialogue, many local dialogues have been and are still held in the southern Philippines. I served as founding director of the Southern Philippine Center for Peace Studies (SPCPS) at Mindanao State University in 1979 and the Xavier Peace Center at Xavier University in Cagayan de Oro City in 1987. The goals of both these peace centers were to involve Christian and Muslim college students in the search for peace in the southern Philippines. Both peace centers sponsored several conferences and local dialogues on improving relations between Muslims and Christians in the southern Philippines. At several weekend live-in dialogues of college students, there were hostile feelings and expressions exchanged between Muslims and Christians in the opening sessions. By the close of the dialogues, these students formed and expressed warm friendship for each other. They did not agree on all issues, but they did agree to try to resolve their differences in a rational, peaceful manner.

After several Muslim-Christian College Students Peace Conferences were held in various schools in Mindanao, they all issued recommendations to the government and religious leaders to improve relationships between the Muslims and Christians in the southern Philippines. Another result was the formation of College Peace Clubs in Mindanao that continued to meet on the local and regional level. Other peace dialogues, conferences, and seminars were organized and implemented by SPCPS, MSU, and Xavier University until the 1990s. They are no longer functional and are in need of revival. The fighting/conflict between the MNLF and MILF against the AFP has diminished, but the misunderstanding and prejudice between Muslims and Christians need much attention and improvement. In the closing months of 1999, both the MNLF and the MILF are threatening to resume hostilities unless the autonomy issue is decided in their favor. This would be a tragedy of major proportions that would hurt the entire Philippines, but the Muslims will continue to suffer the most.

Muslim-Christian dialogue in the Philippines has been going on at the formal and informal level since the 1960s. Dialogues have been sponsored by the GRP, by church organizations, and by the Muslim *ummah*. There has been much improvement in understanding and relationships between Muslims and Christians who have been involved in dialogues. Attitudes have been changed, stereotypes have been removed, and new friendships have been formed. Surely all will agree that dialogue is much to be preferred over confrontation, antipathy, and *apartheid*.

The media continue to report the bad news of violence, bombings, and kidnappings in the southern Philippines. Dialogues, friendships, and goodwill between Muslims and Christians are not exciting to the newspapers. In the continuing search for peace in the southern Philippines, Muslim-Christian dialogue at all levels has demonstrated that it can produce better understanding and the hope for peace, development, and prosperity for all the people of the southern Philippines — and for all the Malays of Southeast Asia.

D. A Malaysian Christian Response

Canon Sadayandy Batumalai is a Malaysian Christian of Hindu Indian heritage. He is Dean of Seminari Theoloji in Kuala Lumpur. Canon Batumalai has written *A Malaysian Theology of Muhibbah*, "A Theology for a Christian Witnessing in Malaysia." "Muhibbah" means "goodwill" and comes from the Arabic "muhabbat" which means "love" or "affection." Jesus Christ is understood as Utusan Muhabbat or "goodwill mission." Both God's will and goodwill are intrinsically related to one another. The gospel presupposes goodwill (Batumalai, 1990: 1).

Canon Batumalai suggests that the Christian response to our Muslim neighbor will follow the example of Jesus in the story of the Good Samaritan. The Christian will love God with all his heart, mind, and strength, and he will love his Muslim neighbor as he loves himself. Batumalai believes that the Great Commandment — to love God *and* your neighbor — must be taken seriously before the Christian can fulfill the Great Commission — making disciples of all nations.

The first response of Malaysian Christians to Islamic resurgence is to better understand their Malay Muslim neighbors. This will lead to a sympathetic understanding of their problems and needs. This can help to bring down walls of division and promote national unity. Malaysian Christians must identify themselves as Malaysian citizens and disciples of Jesus Christ. Christian unity is important in achieving national unity. The church, which is almost 7 percent of the total population, must seek new opportunities for service to the nation to promote spiritual welfare. The church can enhance its status by using Bahasa Malay instead of English, Chinese, or Tamil. In this way the gospel can be presented to Muslims. Muslims and Christians in Malaysia are to seek a basis for friendship in forming a Muslim-Christian community (Batumalai, 1990: 89-91).

Batumalai says that while formal interreligious dialogue may not be possible in Malaysia at the present time, dialogue of life, dialogue of deeds, dialogue of words, and dialogue of religious experience can be implemented. Dialogue is a way of relating to our neighbor of other faiths. "True dialogue with a man of another faith requires a concern both for the Gospel and for the other man. The love of God and the love of neighbor is underlined in this concern" (Batumalai, 1990: 114-17). In short, dialogue is muhibbah in action.

The word "Muslim" means "one who submits his entire life to the will of God." The Christian prays, "Thy will be done on earth, as it is in heaven." Both faithful Christians and faithful Muslims want to follow God's will in their daily lives. What is God's will for all the Malays in Southeast Asia? Are Malay Muslims and Malay Christians ready to seek God's will together? This can be done on a government-to-government basis through ASEAN and other meetings. It can also be done on a community-to-community basis and a person-to-person basis. Muslim and Christian religious leaders and communities can contribute their answers through dialogue. The future of Malay Southeast Asia is bright indeed if Muslims and Christians of goodwill work together to solve the problems of this area. Together they can see their hopes and dreams become a reality for themselves and their children. *Inshallah.* God's will be done.

Bibliography

Abbott, Walter M., S.J., Editor.
1966   *The Documents of Vatican II.* New York: American Press.

Abdullah, Taufik.
1978   "Identity Maintenance and Identity Crisis in Minangkabau." In *Identity and Religion: International, Cross-Cultural Approaches.* Edited by Hans Mol. London/Beverly Hills, Calif.: Sage Publications Inc., 151-68.

Abdullah, Taufik, and Sharon Siddique, Editors.
1986   *Islam and Society in Southeast Asia.* Singapore: Institute of Southeast Asian Studies.

Addison, James Thayer.
1942   *The Christian Approach to the Moslem.* New York: Columbia University Press.

Afable, Lourdes B.
1960   "The Muslims as an Ethnic Minority in the Philippines," *Philippine Sociological Review* 8: 16-23.

Agoncillo, Teodoro A., and Oscar M. Alfonso.
1960   *A Short History of the Filipino People.* Manila: University of the Philippines.

Ahmad, Hussein S.
1988   "Islam and Politics in Malaysia." Ph.D. Thesis, Yale University.

Ahmad, Muhammad Saleem.
1980   "Islam in Southeast Asia: A Study of the Emergence and Growth in Malaysia and Indonesia," *Islamic Studies* 19, no. 2 (Summer): 134-41.

Al-Attas, Syed Naguib.
1963   *Some Aspects of Sufism as Understood and Practised Among the Malays.* Edited by Shirle Gordon. Singapore: Malaysian Sociological Research Institute Ltd.

Aliran Speaks.
1977-81   Penang, Malaysia: Aliran Kasedaran Negara.

Allen, E. L.
1960   *Christianity Among the Religions.* London: George Allen and Unwin Ltd.

Anderson, J. N. D., Editor.
1960   *The World's Religions.* Grand Rapids: Eerdmans.

Andrae, Tor.
1936   *Mohammed: The Man and His Faith.* Translated by Theophel Menzel. London: George Allen and Unwin Ltd.

Angeles, F. Delor.
1964   *Mindanao: The Story of an Island.* Davao City, Philippines: San Pedro Press, Inc.

Anwar, Khaidir.
1979   "Islam in Indonesia Today," *The Islamic Quarterly* 23, no. 2: 99-102.

Anwar, Zainah.
1987   *Islamic Revivalism in Malaysia: Dakwah Among the Students.* Selangor, Malaysia: Pelanduk Publications.

Arberry, A. J.
1944   *The Koran Interpreted.* New York: Macmillan.

Archer, R. L.
1937   "Muhammadan Mysticism in Sumatra," *Journal of the Malayan Branch of the Royal Asiatic Society* 15, no. 2: 1-126.

Arnold, Sir Thomas W.
1913   *The Preaching of Islam.* London: Constable and Company, Inc.

Asani, Abdul Razak.
1988   "The Bangsamoro People," *Journal Institute of Muslim Minority Affairs,* 296-310.

Asiaweek.
1994   August 17. "Tightening the Screws," 28; "To Veil or Not to Veil," 30-31.

Avila, John Lawrence.
1990   "A Gathering Crisis in the Philippines." *Southeast Asian Affairs 1990.* Singapore: Institute of Southeast Asian Studies, 255-73.

Ayoob, Mohammed.
1981   *The Politics of Islamic Reassertion.* New York: St. Martin's Press.
1990   *India and Southeast Asia: Indian Perceptions and Policies.* London & New York: Routledge (Published under the auspices of the Institute of Southeast Asian Studies, Singapore).

Bakar, Mohamad Abu.
1981   "Islamic Revivalism and the Political Process in Malaysia," *Asian Survey* 21, no. 10 (October): 1040-59.

Bakker, D.
1913   "The Desire for Higher Civilization and the Spread of Islam in Java," *Moslem World* 3: 248-54.
1972   "The Struggle for the Future: Some Significant Aspects of Contemporary Islam in Indonesia," *Muslim World* 62: 126-36.

Banks, David J.
1976   "Islam and Inheritance in Malaya: Culture Conflict or Islamic Revolution?," *American Ethnologist* 3, no. 4 (November): 573-86.
1982   "The Role of Spirit Beliefs and Islam in the 20th Century Malay Villagers' Idea of Ultimate Reality," *Ultimate Reality and Meaning* 5, no. 4: 314-27.

Barber, W. T. A.
1915   "Raymond Lull," *Moslem World* 5: 118-23.

Barny, Fred J.
1941   "The Fourth Grace — Endurance," *Muslim World* 31: 1-4.

Barraclough, Simon.
1983   "Managing the Challenges of Islamic Revival in Malaysia," *Asian Survey* 33, no. 8 (August): 958-78.

Batumalai, Sadayandy.
1990   *A Malaysian Theology of Muhibbah.* Kuala Lumpur, Malaysia.
1994   "Malaysian Islamic Situation and a Response from a Malaysian Christian Perspective," *Bulletin of the Commission on Theological Concerns* 12 (January-July), Christian Conference of Asia.

Beaver, R. Pierce.
1964   *From Missions to Mission.* New York: Association Press.

Benda, Harry J.
1955   "Indonesian Islam under the Japanese Occupation, 1942-45," *Pacific Affairs* 28, no. 4: 350-62.
1965   "Continuity and Change in Indonesian Islam," *Asian and African Studies* 1: 123-38.

Bennett, Russell L.
1964   "Notes on Two Years Among the Maranao," *Silliman Journal* 11 (July-September): 217-37.

Berreman, Gerald D.
1965   "The Philippines: A Survey of Current Social, Economic and Political Conditions." Data Paper: November 19, Southeast Asia Program, Department of Far Eastern Studies. Ithaca, N.Y.: Cornell University.

Bethmann, Erich W.
1953   *Bridge to Islam.* London: George Allen and Unwin Ltd.

Beyer, H. O., and Holleman, F. D.
n.d.   "Beyer-Holleman Collection of Original Sources in Philippine Customary Law." Unpublished Manuscript, Library of Congress, Washington, D.C.; and the Philippines Studies Program, University of Chicago.

Beyer, H. Otley, and De Vera, Jaime C.
1947   *Philippine Saga.* Manila: *The Evening News.*

Blair, Emma Helena, and James Alexander Robertson, Editors.
1909   *The Philippine Islands, 1493-1803.* 55 vols. Cleveland: A. H. Clark Company.

Blasdell, R. A.
1942   "How Islam Came to the Malay Peninsula," *Moslem World* 32: 114-21.

Boland, B. J., and I. Farjon.
1983   *Islam in Indonesia: A Bibliographical Survey 1600-1942 with Post-1945 Addenda.* Foris Publications: Holland and U.S.A.

Bordewich, Fergus M.
1995   "A Holy War Heads West," *Reader's Digest* (January), 73-78.

Bosquet, G. H.
1940   *A French View of the Netherland Indies.* Translated from the French by Philip E. Lilienthal. London: Oxford University Press.

Cahen, Claude.
1965   *Jean Sauvaget's Introduction to the History of the Muslim East: A Bibliographical Guide.* Berkeley and Los Angeles: University of California Press.

Cantilevers.
1999   "The Two Sacred Paths: Christianity and Islam." (Spring).

Chandra, Dilip.
1971   "Islam in Modern Indonesia," *Islam and the Modern Age* 2, no. 4: 96-108.

Che Man, W. K.
1990   *Muslim Separatism: The Moros of Southern Philippines and Malays of Southern Thailand.* Manila: Ateneo de Manila Press.

Chelliah, V. A., and Alexander McLeish.
n.d.   *Malaya and Singapore.* London: World Dominion Press.

Cherry, W. T.
1935   "British Malaya as a Mission Field" (A summary based on the 1921 Census), *Muslim World* 13: 30-38.

Christians Meeting Muslims.
1977   *WCC Papers on Ten Years of Dialogue,* World Council of Churches, Geneva.

Christian Mission and Islamic Da'wah.
1982/1402H   Leicester, U.K.: The Islamic Foundation.

Cole, Fay-Cooper.
1945   *The Peoples of Malaysia.* New York: D. van Nostrand Company, Inc.

Conference on the Tripoli Agreement.
1985   International Studies Institute of the Philippines.

Corpuz, O. D.
1989   *The Roots of the Filipino Nation.* Quezon City, Philippines: AKLAHI Foundation, Inc., I & II.

Costa, H. De La, S.J.
1961   *The Jesuits in the Philippines, 1581-1768.* Cambridge, Mass.: Harvard University Press.
1964   "Muhammad Alimuddin I, Sultan of Sulu, 1735-1773." Unpublished manuscript presented as Paper No. 80 at the International Conference on Asia History, University of Hong Kong (August 30-September 5).

Cowan, C. O., and O. W. Walters, Editors.
1976   *Southeast Asian Historiography: Essays Presented to D. C. E. Hall.*

Coward, Howard.
1985   *Pluralism.* New York: Orbis Books.

Cragg, Kenneth.
1970   *Alive to God: Muslim and Christian Prayer.* New York: Oxford University Press.
1975   *The House of Islam.* Belmont, Calif.: Wadsworth Publishing.
1985   *The Call of the Minaret.* Maryknoll, N.Y.: Orbis.

Crawfurd, John.
1820   *History of the Indian Archipelago.* 3 vols. Edinburgh: Archibald Constable and Company.

Crouch, H.
1988   "Indonesia: The Rise and Fall of Suharto's Generals," *Third World Quarterly* 10: 160-75.

Das, Parimal Kumar.
1987   *The Troubled Region: Issues of Peace and Development in Southeast Asia.* New Delhi: Sage Publications.

Davies, I. Talog.
n.d.   "Malay as Defined in the States Malay Reservation Enactments," *Intisari* 1, no. 1: 27-28.

Delius, Eberhard.
1935   "The Spirit of Islam in Sumatra," *Moslem World* 25: 145-55.

Development of Islam in Indonesia.
1980   Published by the Office of Islamic Information Service, The Ministry of Religious Affairs of the Republic of Indonesia. January: P. T. Karya Uni Press.

Docummun, Dolores.
1962   "Sisangat: A Fishing Village of Sulu," *Philippine Sociological Review* 10 (July-October): 91-106.

D'Souza, Andreas.
1991   "Resurgent Islam: Its Political Implications for Asia." Islam in Asia Consultation. Bangkok: Lutheran World Federation.

Elert, Werner.
1962   *The Structure of Lutheranism.* Vol. 1. Translated by Walter Hansen. St. Louis: Concordia Publishing House.

Engineer, Asghar Ali.
1985   *Islam in South and Southeast Asia.* Delhi: Ajanta Publications.

Esposito, John L., Editor.
1987   *Islam in Asia: Religion, Politics, and Society.* New York and Oxford: Oxford University Press.

Esposito, John L.
1992   *Islam: The Straight Path.* New York: Oxford University Press.

Fatimi, S. Q.
1963   *Islam Comes to Malaysia.* Edited by Shirle Gordon. Singapore: Malaysian Sociological Research Institute, Ltd.

Federspiel, Howard M.
1973   "The Military and Islam in Sukarno's Indonesia," *Pacific Affairs* 46, no. 3 (Fall): 407-20.

Ferrer, Miriam Coronel, Editor.
1997   *Peace Matters: A Philippine Peace Compendium.* Quezon City: University of the Philippines.

Filipino Muslims.
1964-65   *Hibbert Journal* 63: 39-41.

Fitz, Angelika.
1982   "Islamic Parties and the Struggle to Determine the Character of the State of Indonesia." In *Islamic Studies in the German Democratic Republic.* Edited by Holger Preisler and Martin Robbe, in issue of the *Asia, Africa, Latin America Journal.* Berlin: Akademie-Verlag, 61-75.

Fitzgerald, Michael L.
1976   "Christian-Muslim Dialogue in Southeast Asia," *Islamo-Christiana* 2: 171-85.

Forbes, W. Cameron.
1928   *The Philippine Islands.* 2 vols. Boston: Houghton Mifflin.

Fox, R. B.
1957   "A Consideration of Theories Concerning Possible Affiliations of Mindanao Culture with Borneo, the Celebes, and Other Regions of the Philippines," *Philippine Sociological Review,* 2-12.

Funston, John.
1981   "Malaysia." In *The Politics of Islamic Reassertion*. Edited by Ayoob Moham-
        med. New York: St. Martin's Press, 165-89.

Furnivall, J. S.
1941   *Progress and Welfare in Southeast Asia*. New York: Institute of Pacific Rela-
        tions.

Gale, Bruce, Editor.
1986   *Readings in Malaysian Politics*. Selangor, Malaysia: Pelanduk Publications.

Gallagher, Charles F.
1966   "Islam in Politics: Southeast Asia," *Muslim World* 66: 257-62.

Garcia, Ed, and Carol Hernandez, Editors.
1989   "Waging Peace in the Philippines." (Proceedings of the 1988 International
        Conference on Conflict Resolution.) Metro Manila: Ateneo de Manila and
        University of the Philippines.

Geertz, Clifford.
1960   *The Religion of Java*. New York: Free Press.
1963   "Modernization in a Moslem Society: The Indonesian Case," *Quest* 39 (Octo-
        ber-November): 9-17.

Gibb, H. A. R.
1949   *Mohammedanism*. London: Oxford University Press.

Ginsburg, Norton, and Chester F. Roberts, Jr.
1958   *Malaya*. Seattle: University of Washington.

Glazer, S.
1941   "The Moros as a Political Factor in Philippine Independence," *Pacific Affairs*
        14: 78-90.

Gomez, Hilario M.
1977   "The Muslim Filipino Rebellion," Ph.D. Thesis. Princeton University.

Gordon, Shirle.
n.d.   "Editorial," *Intisari* 1: 3-4.

Gowing, Peter G.
1964[a]   *Mosque and Moro: A Study of Muslims in the Philippines*. Manila: Philippine
        Federation of Christian Churches.
1964[b]   "Islam: The Contemporary Scene," *Philippine Studies* 12 (October): 639-47.
1964[c]   "Muslim Filipinos Today," *Muslim World* 64: 39-48, 112-21.

1965   "Kris and Crescent," *Aramco World* 16 (July-August): 2-11.

1977[a]   "Past and Present Posture in Christian-Muslim Relations in Insular Southeast Asia," *Southeast Asia Journal of Theology* 18, no. 1: 33-44.

1977[b]   *Mandate in Moroland: The American Government of Muslim Filipinos 1899-1920.* Quezon City: New Day Publishers.

1978   "Christian-Muslim Relations in the Philippines," *Southeast Asia Journal of Theology* 19, no. 2: 1-13.

1979[a]   "The Moro Rebellion: Why and Wherefore," Newsletter of Centre for the Study of Islam and Christian-Muslim Relations, no. 2 (September).

1979[b]   *Muslim Filipinos: Heritage and Horizon.* Quezon City: New Day Publishers.

1981   "Christian-Muslim Dialogue in the Philippines: 1976-1981," *Islamo-Christiana* 7: 211-25.

1982[a]   "Religion and Regional Cooperation: The Mindanao Problem and ASEAN." Paper read at Sixth Seminar on Religion as a Field of Study and Research. Sponsored by the Ministry of Religious Affairs, Jakarta, Indonesia (March 1982).

1982[b]   "The Muslim Filipino Minority." In *The Crescent in the East.* Edited by Rafael Israeli. London & Dublin: Curzon Press.

1988   *Understanding Islam and Muslims in the Philippines.* Manila: New Day Publishers.

Gowing, Peter G., and Robert D. McAmis, Editors.

1974   *Muslim Filipinos.* Manila: Solidaridad Publishers.

Guidelines for Dialogue Between Muslims and Christians.

1969   Rome: Secretarius Pro Non-Christians.

Guidelines for Dialogue with People of Living Faiths and Ideologies.

1979   Geneva: World Council of Churches.

Guillaume, Alfred.

1956   *Islam.* Baltimore: Penguin Books.

Hall, D. G. E., Editor.

1961   *Historians of South East Asia.* London: Oxford University Press.

Hall, D. G. E.

1981   *A History of South East Asia.* New York: St. Martin's Press.

Hamid, Ismail.

1983   *The Malay Islamic Hikayat.* Bangs Selangor, Malaysia: Penerbit University Kebangsaan Malaysia.

Hamka.
1978   "Developments in Islam." In *Malaysia 2001*. Edited by Bruce-Ross Larson. Kuala Lumpur: Syed Kechick Foundation.

Harrison, Tom.
1956   "'Bisaya': Borneo-Philippine Impacts of Islam," *Sarawak Museum Journal* 7 (June): 43-47.

Hassan, Prof. Madya Dr. Kamal.
1981   *Islamic Identity Crisis in the Muslim Community in Contemporary Malaysia.* Kuala Lumpur: Pustaka Ilmu Raya.

Hefner, Robert W.
1987   "Islamizing Java? Religion and Politics in Rural East Java," *The Journal of Asian Studies* 46, no. 3 (August): 533-54.

Hinkhouse, Paul McClure.
1919   "Islam in Siam," *Moslem World* 9: 142-48.

Hodgson, Marshall G. S.
1974   *The Venture of Islam.* 3 vols. Chicago: University of Chicago Press.

Hooker, M. B., Editor.
1983   *Islam in Southeast Asia.* Leiden: E. J. Brill.

Hourani, George F.
1951   *Arab Seafaring.* Princeton, N.J.: Princeton University Press.

Hunt, Chester L.
1955   "Moslems and Christians in the Philippines," *Pacific Affairs* 28: 331-49.

Hurgronje, C. Snouck.
1906   *The Achehnese.* 2 vols. Leyden: E. J. Brill.

Hurley, Victor.
1936   *The Swish of the Kris: The Story of the Moros.* New York: E. P. Dutton Company.

Hussein, S. Ahmad.
1988   *Islam and Politics in Malaysia, 1969-1982: The Dynamics of Competing Traditions.* Ann Arbor, Mich.: University Microfilms International.

Ibrahim, Ahmad.
1981   "Islamic Law in Malaysia," *Jernal Undang-Undang*, 8, parts 1 & 2: 21-57.

Ibrahim, Ahmad, Sharon Siddique, and Yasim Hussain, Compilers.
1985   *Readings on Islam in Southeast Asia.* Singapore: Institute of Southeast Asian Studies.

Ibrahim bin Safie.
1981   *The Islamic Party of Malaysia: Its Formative Stages and Ideology.* Kelantan, Malaysia: Nuawi Bin Ismail.

Index Islamics 1906-1955.
1958   Compiled by J. D. Pearson with the assistance of Julia F. Ashton. Cambridge: W. Heffer & Sons Ltd.

Index Islamicus Supplement: 1956-1960.
1962   Compiled by J. D. Pearson. Cambridge: W. Heffer & Sons Ltd.

Index Islamicus: 1976-1980.
1983   Compiled by J. D. Pearson. London: Mansell Publishing; Part 2, Monographs. Compiled by J. D. Pearson and Wolfgang Behr. London: Mansell Publishing Ltd.

Index Islamicus: 1981-1990.
1982   VI No. 4. Compiled by W. A. Lockwood & G. J. Roper.
1981-90   V-XIV. Edited by J. D. Pearson. London: Mansell Publishing Ltd.

"Integration of the Muslims."
1957   *Philippine Journal of Education* 35 (March): 617.

International Seminar on Islam in Southeast Asia.
1986   Djakarta: Lembaga Penelitian Iain Syarif Hidayatullah.

Isidro, Antonio, and Mamitua Saber, Editors.
1968   *Muslim Philippines.* University Research Center, Marawi City, Philippines.

Israeli, Raphael, Editor.
1982   *The Crescent in the East.* London and Dublin: Curzon Press.

Israeli, Raphael, and Anthony H. Johns, Editors.
1984   *Islam in Asia.* Vol. 2. *Southeast and East Asia.* Jerusalem: The Magnes Press, Hebrew University.

Jackson, Karl D.
1980   *Traditional Authority, Islam and Rebellion: A Study of Indonesian Political Behavior.* Berkeley, Los Angeles, London: University of California Press.

Johns, A. H.

1981   "From Coastal Settlement to Islamic School and City: Islamization in Suma-
        tra, the Malay Peninsula and Java," *Hamdard Islamicus* 4, no. 4 (Winter): 3-28.

Jones, L. Bevan.

1952   *Christianity Explained to Muslims.* Calcutta: Y.M.C.A. Publishing House.
1959   *The People of the Mosque.* Calcutta: Baptist Mission Press.

Joseph, John.

1961   *The Nestorians and Their Muslim Neighbors.* Princeton, N.J.: Princeton Uni-
        versity Press.

Journal Institute of Muslim Minority Affairs.

1982-83 Kingdom of Saudi Arabia: King Abdulaziz University, I & II.

Kahane, Reuven.

1984   "Notes on the Unique Patterns of Indonesian Islam," in *Islam in Asia,* Vol. 2.
        Southeast and East Asia. Edited by Raphael Israeli and Anthony H. Johns. Je-
        rusalem: The Magnes Press, Hebrew University.

Karnow, Stanley, and the Editors of *Life.*

1964   "South-East Asia." Amsterdam: Time-Life International.

Kennedy, D. J.

1912   "Thomas Aquinas, Saint," *The Catholic Encyclopedia* XIV. New York: Robert
        Appleton Company.

Kettani, M. Ali, Editor.

1986   *Muslim Minorities in the World Today.* London and New York: Mansell Pub-
        lishing Limited.

Kittler, Glenn D.

1951   *The White Fathers.* New York: Harper and Brothers.

Kraemer, Hendrik.

1923   "Missionary Work in Java," *Moslem World* 13 (July): 263-69.
1937   "A Survey of the Netherlands Indies," *Moslem World* 27: 44-55.
1938   *The Christian Message in a Non-Christian World.* New York: Harper and
        Brothers.
1958   *From Mission Field to Independent Church.* London: SCM Press Ltd.
1960   "Islamic Culture and Missionary Adequacy," *Muslim World* 50: 244-51.

Latourette, Kenneth Scott.

1937-45 *A History of the Expansion of Christianity.* 7 vols. New York: Harper and
         Brothers.

1958-62 *Christianity in a Revolutionary Age.* 5 vols. New York: Harper and Brothers.

Laubach, Frank C.
1923 "Islam in the Philippines," *Moslem World* 13: 57-66.
1925 *The People of the Philippines.* New York: George H. Doran Company.
1929 "Matias, a Son of Moro Pirates," *Moslem World* 19: 115-24.
1935 "Christianity and Islam in Lanao," *Moslem World* 25: 45-49.

Le Bar, Frank M., Compiler.
n.d. *Insular Southeast Asia: Ethnographic Studies.* New Haven Human Relations Area File.

Lee Yong Leng.
1982 *Southeast Asia: Essays in Political Geography.* Singapore: University Press.

Lewis, Bernard.
1960 *The Arabs in History.* New York and Evanston, Ill.: Harper and Row.

Lim Kit Siang.
1986 *Malaysia: Crisis of Identity.* Petaling Java, Malaysia: Democratic Action Party.

Linga, Abhoud Syed.
1975 Interview with Chairman of Political Section P, MNLF Northern Mindanao, October 1, somewhere in Lanao del Sur, 16.

Lobinger, Charles Summer.
1919 "The Origin of the Moros," *Moslem World* 9: 58-64.

Luther, Martin.
1900 "Das eyn Christliche oder Gemeyne recht und macht Habe," *D. Martin Luthers Werke: Kritische Gesamtausgabe,* XI. Weimar: Herman Bohlaus Nachfolger, 408-16.
1909 "Vom Kriege wider die Tuerken," 1529, *D. Martin Luthers Werke: Kritische Gesamtausgabe,* XXX, ii. Herman Bohlaus Nachfolger, 107-48.
1920[a] "Theodor Biblianders Koranausgabe," Vorrede Luthers, 1543, *D. Martin Luthers Werke: Kritische Gesamtausgabe,* LIII. Weimar: Herman Bohlaus Nachfolger, 569-72.
1920[b] "Verlegung des Alcoran Bruder Richardi Prediger Ordens," Verdeutscht und Herausgegeben durch D. M. Luther, 1542, *D. Martin Luthers Werke: Kritische Gesamtausgabe,* LIII. Weimar: Herman Bohlaus Nachfolger, 272-396.

MacDonald, D. M.
1965 *Development of Muslim Theology, Jurisprudence and Constitutional Theory.* Beyrouth: Khayats.

Madale, A. T.
1957[a]   "Ghost Schools and the Maranaws," *Philippine Journal of Education* 35 (February): 560-61.
1957[b]   "Christmas in the Maranaw Elementary Schools," *Philippine Journal of Education* 36 (December): 426.

Madale, Nagasura T., Editor.
1981   *The Muslim Filipinos.* Quezon City, Philippines: Alemar-Phoenix Publishing House, Inc.

Mahmud, Sayyid Fayyaz.
1960   *A Short History of Islam.* London: Oxford University Press.

Majallatu'l Azhar **(Al-Azhar Magazine)**
1970   English Section edited by A. M. Mohiaddin Alwaye, Cairo.

Majul, Cesar Adib.
1964[a]   "Political and Historical Notes on the Old Sulu Sultanate." Unpublished manuscript presented as Paper No. 30 at the International Conference on Asian History, University of Hong Kong (August 30–September 5).
1964[b]   "Theories on the Introduction and Expansion of Islam in Malaysia," *Silliman Journal* 11: 335-98.
1973   *Muslims in the Philippines.* Quezon City: University of the Philippines Press for the Asian Center.
1976   "An Historical Background on the Coming and Spread of Islam and Christianity in Southeast Asia," *Asian Studies* 14, no. 2: 1-14.
1983   "Islam and Creative Development," *Solidarity* 4: 51-61.
1985   *The Contemporary Muslim Movement in the Philippines.* Berkeley: Mizan Press.
1988   "The Moro Struggle in the Philippines," *Third World Quarterly* (April): 897-922.

Malaysia-Crisis of Identity.
1982   Political Speeches on "Religious Freedom Under Threat" (12/9/82) and "Religious Polarization" (3/13/84), 37-53.

Marasingao, Lakshman.
1986   "The Use of Customary Law in Development in Southeast Asia." In *Religion, Values and Development in Southeast Asia.* Edited by Bruce Matthews and Judith Nagata. Singapore: Institute of Southeast Asian Studies, 22-36.

Marrison, G. E.
1951   "The Coming of Islam to the East Indies," *Journal of the Malayan Branch of the Royal Asiatic Society* 24: 28-37.
1957   "Islam and the Church in Malaya," *Muslim World* 47: 290-98.

Massignon, L.
1915   "The Roman Catholic Church and Islam," *Moslem World* 5: 129-42.

Mastura, Michael O.
1983   "Muslim Law for a Muslim Minority," *Solidarity* 4: 62-72.
1984   *Muslim Filipino Experiences.* New Haven: Yale University Press.

Mathews, Basil.
1944   *Unfolding Drama in Southeast Asia.* New York: Friendship Press.

Matthews, Bruce, and Judith Nagata, Editors.
1986   *Religion, Values and Development in Southeast Asia.* Singapore: Institute of Southeast Asian Studies.

May, R. J.
1984   "The Situation of Philippine Muslims," *Journal Institute of Muslim Minority Affairs.*

McAmis, Robert D.
1973   "Muslim Filipinos in the 1970's," *Solidarity* (December): 3-16.
1976   "An Introduction to the Folk Tales of the Maranao in the Southern Philippines." Transcript Series No. 9 (Philippine Studies Program, University of Chicago).
1983   "Muslim Filipinos in the 1980's," *Solidarity* 4, no. 97: 32-40.
1987   "Inter-religious Dialogue and the Search for Peace in the Southern Philippines," *Dansalan Quarterly* 8, no. 1-2 (December-January): 5-84. Marawi City, Philippines: Gowing Memorial Research Center.

McCutchen, Robert.
1919   "Islam in the Philippine Islands," *Moslem World* 9: 58-64.

McVey, Ruth.
1983   "Faith as the Outsider: Islam in Indonesian Politics." In *Islam in the Political Process.* Edited by James Piscatori. Cambridge: Cambridge University Press.

Mednick, Melvin.
1957   "Some Problems of Moro History and Political Organization," *Philippine Sociological Review* 5: 39-52.
1965   "Encampment of the Lake: The Social Organization of a Moslem-Philippine (Moro) People." Unpublished Ph.D. Thesis, Department of Anthropology, University of Chicago.

Miller, Roland E.
1995   *Muslim Friends: Their Faith and Feelings, an Introduction to Islam.* St. Louis: Concordia Publishing House.

Mills, L. A.
1960   "British Malaya, 1824-67," *Journal of the Malayan Branch, Royal Asiatic Society* 33, part 3, no. 191: 423.

Milner, A. C.
1981   "Islam and Malay Kinship," *Journal of the Royal Asiatic Society* no. 1: 46-61.
1982   *KERAJAAN: Malay Political Culture on the Eve of Colonial Rule.* Tucson: University of Arizona Press.

"Mindanao Papers."
1955   Unpublished manuscript. 2 vols. Philippine Studies Program, University of Chicago.

Mintaredja, H. M. E.
1974   *Islam and Politics: Islam and State in Indonesia.* Djakarta: Silinangi.

Moh(amma)d Rasli bin Moh(amma)d Nawi.
n.d.   "Economic View of Puasa," *Intisari* 1, no. 2: 51-52, 55-57.

Molloy, Ivan.
1983   "The Conflicts in Mindanao. Whilst the Revolution Rolls On, the Jihad Falters." Working Paper No. 30, Department of Government, University of Queensland, Australia, 33.

Morgan, Kenneth W., Editor.
1953   *Islam: The Straight Path.* New York: The Ronald Press Company.

Morris, Eric Eugene.
1988   *Islam and Politics in Aceh.* Ann Arbor, Mich.: University Microfilms.

"Muslim-Christian Young Adults Dialogue."
1978   *Bulletin of Christian Institute for Islamic Studies* 1, no. 3 (January 27-29): 32-37. Marawi City, Philippines: Dansalan Research Center.

Mutalib, Hussain.
1990   *Islam and Ethnicity in Malay Politics.* Singapore: Oxford University Press.

Muzaffar, Chandra.
1987   *Islam Resurgence in Malaysia.* Petaling Java, Malaysia: Penerbit Fajar Bakti Sdn. Bhd.

Nagata, Judith.
1984   *The Reflowering of Malaysian Islam: Modern Religious Radicals and Their Roots.* Vancouver: University of British Columbia Press.
1986   "The Impact of Islamic Revival (Dakwah) on the Religious Culture of Malay-

sia." In *Religion, Values and Development in Southeast Asia.* Edited by Bruce Matthews and Judith Nagata. Singapore: Institute of Southeast Asian Studies, 37-50.

Nakamura, Mitsuo.

1983   *The Crescent Arises over the Banyan Tree: A Study of the Muhammadiyah Movement in a Central Javanese Town.* Yogyakarta, Indonesia: Gadjan Mada University Press.

Nash, Manning.

1987   "Ethnicity in Peninsular Malaysia: The Idiom of Communalism, Confrontation and Cooperation." In *Dimensions of Social Life.* Edited by Paul Hockings. New York; Amsterdam: Mouton de Gruyter, 559-72.

Nasseef, Abdulla Omar.

1986   "Muslim-Christian Relations: The Muslim Approach," *Journal Institute of Muslim Minority Affairs* 7, no. 2 (January): 27-31.

Neill, Stephen.

1966   *Colonialism and Christian Missions.* New York: McGraw-Hill.

Ng Kiok Nam.

1980   "The Situation of Islam in Malaysia."

Nicholson, Clara Kibby.

1965   *The Introduction of Islam into Sumatra and Java: A Study in Cultural Change.* Ann Arbor, Mich.: University Microfilms, Inc.

Nieuwenhuijze, C. A. O. van.

1950   "The Dar ul-Islam Movement in Western Java," *Pacific Affairs* 23, no. 2 (June): 169-83.

1951   "Religious Freedom in Indonesia," *International Review of Missions* 40: 94-103.

1958   *Aspects of Islam in Post-Colonial Indonesia.* The Hague and Bandung: W. Van Hoeve Ltd.

1969   "The Legacy of Islam in Indonesia," *Muslim World* 59: 216-19.

Noble, Lena G.

1977   "The Muslim-Christianity Conflict: Its Religious Background," *Solidarity* 11, no. 2: 18-26.

1981   "Muslim Separation in the Philippines, 1972-1981: The Making of a Stalemate," *Asian Survey* 21, no. 11 (November): 1097-1114.

1983   "Roots of the Bangsa Moro Revolution," *Solidarity* 4: 41-50.

1984   "The Philippines: Autonomy for the Muslims," *Islam in Asia.*

Nor Bin Ngan, Mohd.

1983   *Kitab Jawi: Islamic Thought of the Malay Muslim Scholars.* Singapore: Institute of Southeast Asian Studies.

North, C. R.

1952   *An Outline of Islam.* London: The Epworth Press.

Nortier, C. W.

1924   "Difficulties of Work Among the Javanese," *Moslem World* 14 (July): 273-78.

Ong, M.

1987   "Government and Opposition in Parliamentary." In *Government and Politics in Malaysia.* Edited by Zacharia Haji Ahmad. Singapore: Oxford University Press, 94-110.

O'Shaughnessy, Thomas J., S. J.

1967   "Islam in Southeast Asia," *Studia Missionalia* 16: 55-74.

1970   "Filipino Muslims and National Identity," *Omnis Terra* 25, no. 5 (January): 135-40.

Padwick, Constance.

1961   *Muslim Devotions.* London: S.P.C.K.

Palmier, Leslie H.

1954   "Modern Islam in Indonesia: The Muhammadijah After Independence," *Pacific Affairs* 27, no. 3 (September): 255-63.

Philippines: Repression and Resistance.

1980   London: KSP (Komite ng Sambayang Pilipino), Permanent People's Tribunal Session on the Philippines (PPT).

Pickens, Claude L.

1940   "With the Moros of the Philippines," *Moslem World* 30: 36-40.

1941   "The Moros of the Sulu Sea," *Moslem World* 31: 5-13.

Pickthall, Marmaduke.

1953   *The Meaning of the Glorious Koran.* New York: New American Library.

Piscatori, James P., Editor.

1983   *Islam in the Political Process.* Cambridge: Cambridge University Press.

Prins, J.

1951   "Adatlaw and Muslim Religious Law in Modern Indonesia," *Welt des Islams* 1: 283-300.

Provenchal, Ronald.
1982   "Islam in Malaysia and Thailand." In *The Crescent in the East*. Edited by Raphael Israeli. London and Dublin: Curzon Press.

Qutb, Sayyed.
1977   *Islam and Universal Peace*. Indianapolis: American Trust Publication.

Rahbar, Daud.
1960   *God of Justice*. Leiden: E. J. Brill.

Rahman, Faxlur.
1968   *Islam*. New York: Anchor Books.

Raillon, François.
1989   "Chrétiens et Musulmans en Indonésie: Les Voies de la Tolérance," *Islamo Christiana* 15: 135-67.

Rajashekar, J. Paul, Editor.
1988   *Christian-Muslim Relations in Eastern Africa*. Geneva: Lutheran World Federation.

Ramos, Fidel V.
1996   *Break Not the Peace: The Story of the GRP-MNLF Peace Negotiations, 1992-1996*. Manila: Published by the Friends of Steady Eddie.

Rauws, J.
1911   "Islam and Christianity in Malaysia," *Moslem World* 1: 241-47.

Rauws, John, et al.
1935   *The Netherland Indies*. London and New York: World Dominion Press.

Redfield, Robert.
1956   *The Little Community and Peasant Society and Culture*. Chicago: University of Chicago Press.

Rivera, Generoso F.
1960   "The Maranao Muslims in Lumbayao Lanao," *Philippine Sociological Review* 8 (January-April): 1-9.

Rixhon, Gerard, O.M.I.
1964   "Educational Work in Sulu," *Silliman Journal* 11: 9-56.

Rodriguez, José F.
1963   "The Pendatum Family Is an Example in Religious Tolerance, Harmony," *Manila Bulletin*, December 12, Human Interest Section, 1.

Rosen, Lawrence.
1965   "The Islamization of Indonesia." Unpublished Master's Thesis, University of Chicago.

Rosenthal, Erwin I. J.
1961   *Judaism and Islam.* London: Thomas Yoseloff.

Saber, Mamitua.
1957   "Marginal Leadership in a Culture-Contact Situation." Unpublished Master's Thesis, Department of Sociology and Anthropology, University of Kansas.

Saber, Mamitua, and Charles K. Warriner.
1960   "The Maratabat of the Maranaw," *Philippine Sociological Review* 8 (January-April): 10-15.

Saber, Mamitua, and Mauyag M. Tamano.
1961   "Decision-Making and Social Change in Rural Moroland." Unpublished manuscript, Community Research Council Study Series No. 16. Quezon City: University of the Philippines.

Saleeby, Najeeb M.
1905   *Studies in Moro History, Law and Religion.* Manila: Bureau of Public Printing.
1963   *The History of Sulu.* Manila: Filipiniana Book Guild.

Samartha, S. J.
1971   *Dialogue Between Men of Living Faiths.* Geneva: World Council of Churches.

Samson, Allan A.
1971-72 "Army and Islam in Indonesia," *Pacific Affairs* 44, no. 4 (Winter): 545-65.

Santos, Rufino de Los.
1961   "Developing a Revised Program for the Dansalan Junior College High School, Marawi City, Philippines, on the Basis of Discovered Maranaw Needs." Unpublished Ph.D. Thesis, Columbia University.

SarDesai, D. R.
1989   *Southeast Asia: Past & Present.* San Francisco: Westview Press.

Sather, Clifford A.
1966   "A Letter to Professor Fred Eggan, Philippines Studies Program, University of Chicago," dated April 26, from Peabody Museum, Harvard University.

Schrieke, B.
1955   *Indonesian Sociological Studies.* Bandung: Sumur Bandung.

Schumann, Olaf.
1974   "Islam in Indonesia," *International Review of Missions* 63: 429-38.

Scott, Samuel Bryan (Mrs.).
1913   "Mohammedanism in Borneo," *Journal of the American Oriental Society* 33: 313-44.

Sidjabat, Walter Bonar.
1965   *Religious Tolerance and the Christian Faith: A Study Concerning the Concept of Divine Omnipotence in the Indonesian Constitution in the Light of Islam and Christianity.* Djakarta: Badan Penerbit Kristen.

Simon, Gottfried.
1912   *The Progress and Arrest of Islam in Sumatra.* Translated from the German by E. I. M. Boyd. London, Edinburgh, and New York: Marshall Brothers, Ltd.

Situmpol, Einar, and M. S. Widdwissoeli.
1991[a]   "Christian-Muslim Relations in Indonesia." Islam in Asia Consultation. Bangkok: Lutheran World Federation.
1991[b]   "Islam in Indonesia." Islam in Asia Consultation. Bangkok: Lutheran World Federation.

Smith, Wilfrid.
1957   *Islam in Modern History.* Princeton, N.J.: Princeton University Press.

Soebantardjo, R. M.
1974   "Outline of Indonesian History," *International Review of Missions* 63: 438-44.

Southeast Asian Affairs 1986.
1986   Singapore: Institute of Southeast Asian Studies.

Speight, Marston.
1989   *God Is One: The Way of Islam.* New York: Friendship Press.

Stade, Robert.
1970   *Ninety-nine Names of God in Islam.* Ibadan: Daystar Press.

Stone, Richard L.
1962   "Intergroup Relations Among the Taosug, Samal and Badjao of Sulu," *Philippine Sociological Review* 10 (July-October): 107-33.

"Suharto's Pilgrimage to Mecca: Is There A Subplot?"
1991   *International Herald Tribune* (June 21, 1991), 4.

Suhrke, Astri.
1970-71   "The Thai Muslim: Some Aspects of Minority Integration," *Pacific Affairs* 63, no. 4 (Winter): 531-47.

Sweetman, J. Windrow.
1945-1955 *Islam and Christian Theology.* 2 vols. London: Lutterworth Press.

Tamara, M. Nasir.
1986   *Indonesia in the Wake of Islam.* Kuala Lumpur: The Institute of Strategic and International Studies.

Tan, Samuel Kong.
1974   *The Muslim Armed Struggle in the Philippines, 1900-1941.* Ann Arbor, Mich.: University Microfilms.

Ter Haar, B.
1962   *Adat Law in Indonesia.* Edited and translated from the Dutch by E. Adamson Hoebel and A. Arthur Schiller. Djakarta: Bhratara.

Third World Quarterly.
1988   "Islam and Politics," X. London: Third World Foundation.

Thomas, Ralph B.
1977   "Asia for Asiatics?: Muslim Filipino Response to Japanese Occupation and Propaganda during World War II," *Occasional Papers* 7 (May): 32. Marawi City, Philippines: Dansalan Research Center.

Tibbetts, G. R.
1957   "Early Muslim Traders in Southeast Asia," *Journal of the Malayan Branch of the Royal Asiatic Society* 30: 1-45.

Tisdall, Chas. E. G.
1911   "A Plea for the Malays," *Moslem World* 1: 170-74.

Trocki, Carl A.
1980   "Islam: Threat to ASEAN Regional Unity?" *Current History* 18, no. 456 (April): 149-53, 181-82.

Van der Kroef, Justin M.
1953   "The Arabs in Indonesia," *Middle East Journal* 7: 300-323.
1954   "Communism and Islam in Indonesia: A Western View," *India Quarterly* 10: 314-52.
1960   "Problems of Dutch Mission Policy in Indonesia," *Practical Anthropology* 7: 263-72.
1962   "Recent Trends in Indonesian Islam," *Muslim World* 62: 48-58.

n.d.   "National and International Dimensions of Indonesian History," *Journal of Southeast Asian History* 6: 17-32.

Van der Meulen, D.
1947   "Muslim Problems Connected with an Independent Indonesia," *Muslim World* 37: 292-300.

Van Dijk, K.
1923   "Muslim Work in Central Java," *Moslem World* 13 (July): 269-76.

Van Kekem, E. G.
1940   "The East Java Mission," *Moslem World* 30: 20-35.

Van Leur, J. C.
1955   *Indonesian Trade and Society.* Bandung: Sumur Bandung.

Van Vactor, Maisie D.
1979   "Resources for the Study of Muslim Filipino at the Dansalan Research Center," *Occasional Papers* 13 (April): 14. Marawi City, Philippines: Dansalan Research Center.

Verdoorn, J. A.
1940   "Fragmenta Islamica," *Moslem World* 30: 171-77.

Villacorta, Wilfrido V.
1989   "The Management of National Security in the Philippines: The Role of Leadership Styles." In *Leadership Perceptions and National Security: The Southeast Asian Experiences.* Edited by Muhammed Ayoob and Chai-anan Samudavanija. Singapore: Institute of Southeast Asian Studies, 57-82.

Vlekke, Bernard H. M.
1943   *Nusantara: A History of the East Indian Archipelago.* Cambridge, Mass.: Harvard University Press.

Von der Mehden, Fred R.
1963   *Religion and Nationalism in Southeast Asia: Burma, Indonesia and the Philippines.* Madison: University of Wisconsin Press.
1968   *Religion and Nationalism in Southeast Asia.* New Haven: Yale University Press.
1986   "The Political and Social Challenge of Islamic Revival in Malaysia and Indonesia," *Muslim World* 76: 219-33.

Von Grunebaum, Gustave E.
1961   *Islam: Essays in the Nature and Growth of a Cultural Tradition.* London: Routledge and Kegan Paul.

Von Ranke, Leopold.
1909   *History of Latin and Teutonic Nations, 1494-1514.* Translated from the German by G. R. Dennis. London: George Bell Sons.

"Waging Peace in the Philippines."
1989   *NDF Draft Program.* Manila: Gintong Tala Publishing House.

Walker, Williston.
1959   *A History of the Christian Church.* Revised by Cyril C. Richardson and others. New York: Scribners.

Warriner, Charles K.
1959   "Myths, Moros, and the Maranaos," *Exchange News Quarterly* 10: 2-3, 20.

Watson, C. R.
1913   "The Moslems of Sumatra as a Type," *Moslem World* 3: 159-60.

Watt, W. Montgomery.
1953   *Muhammad at Mecca.* London: Oxford University Press.
1956   *Muhammad at Medina.* London: Oxford University Press.

Weekes, Richard V.
1984   *Muslim Peoples: A World Ethnographic Survey,* Vol. 11, 953. Westport, Conn.: Greenwood Press.

Widjojoatmodjo, Raden Abdulkadir.
1942   "Islam in the Netherlands East Indies," *The Far Eastern Quarterly* 2: 48-57.

Wilkinson, Richard James.
1906   *Malay Beliefs.* London: Luzac and Company.

Williams, John Alden.
1961   *Islam.* New York: George Braziller.

Winstedt, R. C.
1917   "The Advent of Muhammedanism in the Malay Peninsula and Archipelago," *Journal of the Straits Branch of the Royal Asiatic Society* 62 (December): 171-75.
1920   "The Early Muhammadan Missionaries," *Journal of the Straits Branch of the Royal Asiatic Society* 81 (March): 5-6.
1944   "Indian Influence in the Malay World," *Journal of the Royal Asiatic Society,* London, 186-96.

Wolf, C. U.
1941   "Luther and Muhammedanism," *Moslem World* 31: 161-70.

Yap Kim Hai, Editor.

1980 *Islam's Challenge for Asian Churches.* Papers from a Consultation on "The Challenge of Islam for Asian Churches," 1-50. Singapore: Christian Conference of Asia.

Yegar, Mushe.

1979 *Islam and Islamic Institutions in British Malaya, 1874-1941.* Jerusalem: The Magnes Press, Hebrew University.

Yusuf, Ali.

1978 *The Holy Qur'an: Text, Translation and Commentary.* Washington, D.C.: Islamic Center.

Zaide, Gregorio P.

1949 *Philippine Political and Cultural History.* 2 vols. Manila: Philippine Education Company.

Zaidi, Iqtidar Husain.

1956 "The Muslims in the Philippines." Unpublished Master's Thesis, University of the Philippines.

Zwemer, Samuel M.

1946 *A Factual Survey of the Moslem World.* New York: Fleming H. Revell Company.

Updated Annotated Bibliography

Amdt, Heinz Wolfgang, and Hal Hill, Editors.

1999   *Southeast Asia's Economic Crisis: Origins, Lessons, and the Way Forward.* Singapore: Institute of Southeast Asian Studies.

— An analysis of the financial crisis in Southeast Asia in the latter part of the 1990s. Presents the economic policies that caused the crisis with political repercussions in Indonesia and Thailand leading to attempted bailout by the International Monetary Fund. Includes bibliographical references and index. (LC No. HB3812.568 1999b)

Anwar, Dewi Fortuna.

1994   *Indonesia in ASEAN: Foreign Policy and Regionalism.* Singapore: Institute of Southeast Asian Studies.

— Describes the role of Indonesia in the Association of Southeast Asian Nations. Prepared for Regional Strategic Studies Program. Includes bibliographical references. (LC No. in process)

Ariff, Mohamed, Editor.

1988   *Islamic Banking in Southeast Asia: Islam and the Economic Development of Southeast Asia.* Singapore: Institute of Southeast Asian Studies.

— Papers presented at the Workshop on Islam and the Economic Development of Southeast Asia, held in Singapore from 24 to 26 of June, 1986. Includes bibliographical references. (LC No. HG3290.8.AG185 1988)

1991   *The Islamic Voluntary Sector in Southeast Asia: Islam and the Economic Devel-*

opment of Southeast Asia. Singapore: The Institute of Southeast Asian Studies.

— Describes the role of the voluntary sector of Islam, including *Zakat* and *Waqf* in Indonesia, Malaysia, the Philippines, and Singapore. Includes bibliographical references. (LC No. BP63.A4 S6544 1991)

1998   *APEC and Development Co-operation.* Singapore: Institute of Southeast Asian Studies.

— Present proposal for economic development and cooperation by member nations in the Asia Pacific Economic Cooperation Organization leading to "The Asian Century." Includes bibliographical references and index. (LC No. — not available)

ASEAN Today and Tomorrow

1998   Hanoi: National Political Publishing House.

— A Vietnamese view of the Association of Southeast Asian Nations produced by the National Centre for Social Sciences and Humanities, Institute for Southeast Asian Studies. (LC No. DS520.A874 1998)

Atkinson, Jane Monnig, and Shelly Errington, Editors.

1990   *Power and Difference: Gender in Island Southeast Asia.* Stanford: Stanford University Press.

— Describes role of sexes in Malay world in political and social life. Papers from a conference held at Princeton in December, 1983.

Aziz, Ungku Abdul, Moderator.

1990   *Strategies for Structural Adjustment: The Experience of Southeast Asia.* Washington: International Monetary Fund.

— Papers presented at a seminar held in Kuala Lumpur, Malaysia, June 28-July 1, 1989. Views on economic policies leading to stabilization in Southeast Asia. (LC No. HC441.576 1990)

Baginda, Abdul Razak Abdullah, and Rohana Mahmood, Editors.

1995   *Malaysia's Defense and Foreign Policies.* Petaling Jaya, Selangor Darul Ehsan, Malaysia: Pelanduk Publications.

— Describes role of Malaysian armed forces in the region and in cooperation with the United Nations in Bosnia-Herzegovina. Sponsored by Malaysian Strategic Research Centre. Papers by Mahathir Mohamad and Anwar Ibrahim. Includes bibliographical references.

Barbier, Jean Paul, and Douglas Newton, Editors.

1989   *Islands and Ancestors: Indigenous Styles of Southeast Asia.* Munich, Germany: Prestel.

— Catalog of an exhibition at the Metropolitan Museum of Art, New York, dealing with folk art, social life, and customs of the Malays. (LC No. GN635.S58 178 1989)

Bin Abu Bakar, Ibrahim, Editor.
1996   *Essays on Muslim Theology and Philosophy.* Bangi Selangor, Malaysia: Jabatan Usuludoin dan Falasafah, Fakulti Pengajian Islam, Universiti Kebangsaan Malaysia.

— Proceedings of the International Seminar on Islamic Theology and Philosophy held at Universiti Kebangsaan Malaysia, June 10-12, 1996. In English, with some articles in Arabic. Includes bibliographical references. (LC No. BP166.166 1996)

Brown, David.
1994   *The State and Ethnic Politics in Southeast Asia.* London, New York: Routledge.

— Covers the minorities, politics, and government of entire Southeast Asian nations with emphasis on ethnic relations. Includes bibliographical references. (LC No. DS526.7.B76 1994)

Budiman, Arief, Editor.
1990   *State and Civil Society in Indonesia.* Clayton, Victoria, Australia: Centre of Southeast Asian Studies, Monash University.

— Papers on the history, social conditions, and economics of Indonesia. Includes bibliographical references.

Cato, Robert.
1996   *Moro Swords.* Singapore: Graham Brash.

— Glimpses into the violent struggle of various Muslim groups in the southern Philippines. Includes bibliographical references. (LC No. U856.P6 C37 1996)

Chee, Stephen, Editor.
1991   *Leadership and Security in Southeast Asia.* Singapore: Institute of Southeast Asian Studies.

— Concerned with issues of leadership and national security in Indonesia, Malaysia, Philippines, Singapore, and Thailand. Includes bibliographical references. (LC No. UA830.L37 1991)

Choudhury, Masudul Alam.
1993   *Theory and Practice of Islamic Development Co-operation: Recent Experience of Some Asian Countries.* Ankara, Turkey: Statistical, Economic, and Social Research Training Centre for Islamic Countries.

— Details of economic aspects, policies, development, integration, and international cooperation with emphasis on Bangladesh, Indonesia, and Malaysia. Includes bibliographical references. (LC No. HC440.8.C474 1993)

Christie, Clive J.
1998   *Southeast Asia in the Twentieth Century: A Reader.* London, New York: Tauris.

— History of mainland and insular Southeast Asia focused on twentieth century. Includes bibliographical references. (LC No. DS526.6.C47 1998)

Church, Peter C., Editor.
1995   *Focus on Southeast Asia.* St. Leonards, Australia: Allen & Unwin.

— A history of Southeast Asia produced by ASEAN Focus Group describing political and economic conditions. Includes bibliographical references. (LC No. DS525.F63 1995)

Committee on Women's Studies in Asia, Editors.
1994   *Women's Studies, Women's Lives: Theory and Practice in South and Southeast Asia.* New Delhi: Kali for Women.

— Essays on the impact of women's studies on their lives by various women's studies scholars from Asia. Includes bibliographical references. (LC No. HQ1181.14 W68 1994)

Corden, Warner Max.
1999   *The Asian Crisis: Is There a Way Out?* Singapore: Institute of Southeast Asian Studies.

— Reveals how the International Monetary Fund responded to the financial and foreign exchange crisis in Southeast Asia in the latter part of the 1990s. Includes bibliographical references. (LC No. HB3808.C67 1999)

Crouch, Harold A.
1988   *The Army and Politics in Indonesia.* Ithaca, N.Y.: Cornell University Press.

— Describes the strong influence of the Indonesian military in the government during the period of presidents Sukarno and Suharto. Bibliography. (LC No. DS644.C76 1988)

Dahm, Bernhard, and Gotz Link, Editors.
1988   *Culture and Technological Development in Southeast Asia.* Baden-Baden, Germany: Nomos.

— German scholars demonstrate the role of technology on social life and civilization throughout Southeast Asia. Bibliography. (LC No. DS523.2.C85 1988)

Daim bin Zainuddin.
1990   *ASEAN Economic Cooperation: Agenda for the 1990's.* Singapore: Institute of Southeast Asian Studies.

— A report of the ASEAN Economic Research Unit on the economic policies of the members of the Association of Southeast Asian Nations. (LC No. DS441.D35 1990)

Dhofier, Zamakhsyari.

1999   *The Pesantren Tradition: The Role of the Kyai in the Maintenance of Traditional Islam in Java.* Tempe, Ariz.: Monograph Series Press. Program for Southeast Asian Studies, Arizona State University.

— An English translation of the author's 1980 Ph.D. thesis at the Australian National University about the influence of one of the major factors on the heavily populated Indonesian Island of Java. Describes the traditions, history, education, and religion of the Javanese. Bibliography. (LC No. in process)

Dictionaries in the Language of Southeast Asian Countries.

1991   Canberra, Australia: Asian Collection Section, National Library of Australia.

— Contains a selected Bibliography based on the collections of the National Library of Australia. (LC No. 23221.N38 1991)

Disoma, Esmail R.

1990   *The Meranao: A Study of Their Practices and Beliefs.* Marawi City, Philippines: Department of Sociology, College of Social Sciences and Humanities, Mindanao State University.

— Ethnology of the Maranao Muslim Group of Central Mindanao from a Maranao perspective. Includes bibliographical references. (LC No. DS666.M37 D57 1990)

Dolcina, Donatella, and Francesco Montessoro.

1997   *India in the Islamic Era and Southeast Asia (Eighth to Nineteenth Century).* Austin, Tex.: Raintree Steck-Vaughn. English translation by Pamela Swinglehurst.

— Provides an overview of the history of India and Southeast Asia with an emphasis on the extensive Indian influence on the development of Islam in the Malay world. (LC No. DS452.D6513 1997)

Dorst, Jean.

1989   *Southeast Asia.* Milwaukee: Raintree Publishers.

— Describes the natural and ecological riches, boundaries, and life of the wild habitat of Southeast Asia. In the World Nature Encyclopedia series. (LC No. QH193.S59 D6713 1989)

Drabble, John H.

1989   *The Emergence of the Modern Malayan Economy: The Impact of Foreign Trade in the Nineteenth Century.* Clayton, Australia: Monash University, Centre of Southeast Asian Studies.

— Title is self-explanatory. Describes commerce and economic conditions in Malaysia. (LC No. HC445.5.D73 1989)

Drakard, Jane.

1990   *A Malay Frontier: Unity and Duality in a Sumatran Kingdom.* Ithaca, N.Y.: Southeast Asia Program, Cornell University.

— Based on author's M.A. thesis at Monash University. Presents the influence of Sumatran culture on Indonesian politics, government, and ethnic relations. Includes bibliographical references. (LC No. DS646.15.B29 D7 1990)

Federspiel, Howard M.

1994   *Popular Indonesian Literature of the Qur'an.* Ithaca, N.Y.: Cornell University Press.

— Report on use of Qur'an in teaching and interpretation of Islam. Includes bibliographical references. (LC No. BP130.78.15 F43 1994)

1995   *A Dictionary of Indonesian Islam.* Athens, Ohio: Ohio University Press.

— Information on Bahasa Indonesia and its use in interpretation and explanation of Islam. Includes bibliographical references. (LC No. BP63.15 F43 1995)

Firdausy, Carunia Mulya, Editor.

1998   *International Migration in Southeast Asia: Trends, Consequences, Issues, and Policy Measures.* Djakarta: Southeast Asian Studies Regional Exchange Program: Indonesian Institute of Sciences.

— The relationship between migration and development in Asia and the Pacific with emphasis on Indonesian migration to Malaysia and Australia. Includes bibliographical references. (LC No. JV8490.158 1998)

Gill, Ranjit.

1997   *ASEAN Towards the 21st Century.* London: ASEAN Academic Press.

— A thirty-year history of the Association of South East Asian Nations. (LC No. DS520.G55 1997)

Gomez, Edmund Terence.

1994   *Political Business: Corporate Involvement of Malaysian Political Parties.* Queensland, Australia: James Cook University of North Queensland.

— Shows the relationship between business and government in Malaysia. Includes bibliographical references. (LC No. JQ1062.A979 G65 1994)

Grant, Richard L., Editor.

1993   *China and Southeast Asia: Into the Twenty-First Century.* Honolulu: Pacific Forum; Washington D.C.: Center for Strategic and International Studies.

— Explores future role of the People's Republic with the countries of Southeast Asia. Includes bibliographical references. (LC No. DS525.9.C5 C49 1993)

Halib, Mohammed, and Tim Huxley, Editors.

1998   *Introduction to Southeast Asian Studies.* New York: Saint Martin's Press.

— Acquisition in process; LC No. not available.

Hamzah, B. A., and Mustafa Mohamed Najimudin.

1988   *Development in Southeast Asia: The Challenges.* Kuala Lumpur, Malaysia: Institute of Strategic and International Studies Malaysia.

— Two Malaysians present insights into economic developments in Southeast Asia. Bibliography. (LC No. HC441.B23 1988)

Hefner, Robert W., and Patricia Horvatich, Editors.

1997   *Islam in an Era of Nation States: Politics and Religious Renewal in Muslim Southeast Asia.* Honolulu: University of Hawaii Press.

— Describes involvement of Malay Muslims in national and world politics and the influence of Islamic Fundamentalism. Includes bibliographical references. (LC No. BP173.7.1849 1997)

Hewison, Kevin, Richard Robison, and Garry Rodan, Editors.

1993   *Southeast Asia in the 1990s: Authoritarianism, Democracy and Capitalism.* Australia: Allen & Unwin.

— Concerned with politics, government, and economics throughout the entire Southeast Asian region. Includes bibliographical references. (LC No. JQ96.A91 S68 1993)

Hill, Hal.

1995   *Indonesia's Industrial Policy and Performance: 'Orthodoxy' Vindicated.* Canberra, Australia: Australian National University.

1996   *The Indonesian Economy Since 1966: Southeast Asia's Emerging Giant.* Cambridge and New York: Cambridge University Press.

— Two books by Australian author written while Indonesian economy was growing rapidly before disaster struck in the latter part of 1990s. Both include bibliographical references. (LC Nos. HC441.A1 E284 no.95 and HC441.A1 E284 no. 95 1996)

Hunt, Robert A.

1997   *Islam in Southeast Asia: A Study for Christians.* New York: GBGM Books.

— History and survey of Islam in Asia. Includes bibliographical references. (LC No. BP63.A381&8.6 1997)

Ibrahim, Zawawi.

1998 *The Malay Labourer: By the Window of Capitalism.* Singapore: Institute of Southeast Asian Studies.

— Describes the history and economic conditions of plantation workers in Malaysia and the introduction of labor unions. Includes bibliographical references. (LC No. HD8039.P4692 M49 1998)

International Seminar on Islamic Studies in the ASEAN:
History, Approaches, and Future Trends.

1998 Pattani, Thailand: The College, Prince of Songkla University. Sponsored by the Toyota Foundation.

— Papers presented by several international scholars with emphasis on Malay Muslims in Malaysia, Indonesia, Thailand, and the Philippines, including history and current trends. Includes bibliographical references. (LC No. Microfiche (o)99/63912(B))

Islamic Revitalization in ASEAN Countries.

1989 Proceedings of the third ASEAN Forum for Muslim social scientists, held on September 25-30 at the Institute of Islamic Studies of the University of the Philippines and Mindanao State University, Marawi City.

— Papers on prospects of Malay Islam in insular Southeast Asia. Includes bibliographical references. (LC No. BP63.A4 S6526 1989)

Istiadah.

1995 *Muslim Women in Contemporary Indonesia: Investigating Paths to Resist the Patriarchal System.* Clayton, Victoria, Australia: The Centre of Southeast Asian Studies, Monash University.

— Presents the changing roles of Muslim women in Indonesia with influence of feminism. (LC No. in process)

Jha, Ganganath.

1997 *Ethnic Politics in Southeast Asia and Quest for Identity.* New Delhi: National Book Organization.

— Presents political aspects and prospects of ethnic minorities throughout Southeast Asia. Includes bibliographical references. (LC No. DS523.3.J43 1997)

Jomo, Kwame Sundaram, with Chen Yun Chung (et al.).

1997 *Southeast Asia's Misunderstood Miracle: Industrial Policy and Economic Development in Thailand, Malaysia and Indonesia.* Boulder, Colo.: Westview Press.

— Subtitle is self-explanatory. Written before economic crisis caused problems for "Miracle." Includes bibliographical references. (LC No. HD3616.A775 J66 1997)

Khon, Kim Hoong.

1991   *Malaysia's General Election 1990: Continuity, Change and Ethnic Politics.* Singapore: Institute of Southeast Asian Studies.

— Reveals the political situation in modern Malaysia where the United Malay National Organization (UMNO) is the dominant power under Mahathir Mohammad. Includes bibliographical references. (LC No. JQ719.A55 K48 1991)

Kuhnt-Saptodewo, Sri, Volker Grabowsky, and Martin Grossheim, Editors.

1997   *Nationalism and Cultural Revival in Southeast Asia: Perspectives from the Centre and the Region.* Wiesbaden, Germany: Harrassowitz.

— Presents the post–World War II struggle for independence, nationalism, and ethnicity throughout Southeast Asia. Includes bibliographical references. (LC No. DS525.7.N38 1997)

Laothamatas, Anek, Editor.

1997   *Democratization in Southeast and East Asia.* New York: St. Martin's Press; Singapore: Institute of Southeast Asian Studies.

— Reports from the Conference on Rapid Economic Growth and Democratization in East and Southeast Asia, held in Singapore in 1994. Includes bibliographical references. (LC No. JQ96.A91 D46 1997)

Leake, David, Jr.

1989   *Brunei: The Modern Southeast-Asian Islamic Sultanate.* Jefferson, N.C.: McFarland.

— The story of the oil-rich nation of Brunei and its sultan. Bibliography. (LC No. DS650.3.L43 1989)

Lee, Raymond, Editor.

1986   *Ethnicity and Ethnic Relations in Malaysia.* DeKalb, Ill.: Center for Southeast Asian Studies. Northern Illinois University.

— Title indicates contents. Bibliography. (LC No. DS595.E84 1986)

Lev, Daniel S., and Ruth Thomas McVey, Editors.

1996   *Making Indonesia.* Ithaca, N.Y.: Cornell University.

— Essays on modern Indonesia in honor of George McT. Kahin describing significant aspects of Indonesian history and politics. Includes bibliographical references. (LC No. DS644.M254 1996)

Lim, Patricia Pui Huen, James H. Morrison, and Kwa Chong Guan, Editors.
1998   *Oral History in Southeast Asia: Theory and Method.* Singapore: National Archives of Singapore and Institute of Southeast Asian Studies.

— Compilation of oral folk history that offers insights into culture and lives of common people. Includes bibliographical references. (LC No. DS524.4 O73 1998)

Lim, Patricia Pui Huen, and Triena Noeline Ong, Compilers.
1998   *Institute of Southeast Asian Studies: A Commemorative History, 1968-1998.*

— A history of the Institute that has produced and sponsored research on Southeast Asia with support and influence of the government of Singapore. Includes bibliographical references. (LC No. DS524.8.S55 157 1998)

MacIntyre, Andrew J.
1991   *Business and Politics in Indonesia.* North Sydney, Australia: Allen & Unwin.

— Deals with economic growth in Indonesia and influence of politics and government. Includes bibliographical references. (LC No. JQ759.5.B8 M33 1991)

Mahmood, Rohana, and Thangam Ramnath, Editors.
1992   *Southeast Asia: The Way Forward.* Kuala Lumpur, Malaysia: ISIS Malaysia: Frederick Ebert Stiftung.

— Selected papers from the Fourth Southeast Asia Forum, Kuala Lumpur, January 15-18, 1992. Includes bibliographical references. (LC No. HC411.S685 1992)

McCloud, Donald G.
1995   *Southeast Asia: Tradition and Modernity in the Contemporary World.* Boulder, Colo.: Westview Press.

— History and prospects in the entire region. Includes bibliographical references. (LC No. DS525.M33 1995)

McCoy, Alfred W., Editor.
1998   *Lives at the Margin.* Madison: University of Wisconsin Center for Southeast Asian Studies.

— Library of Congress holdings information not available.

McVey, Ruth Thomas, Editor.
1992   *Southeast Asian Capitalists.* Ithaca, N.Y.: Southeast Asia Program, Cornell University.

— Story of investors and financiers throughout Southeast Asia. Includes bibliographical references. (LC HC441.S73 1992)

Montes, Manuel F.
1998   *The Currency Crisis in Southeast Asia.* Singapore: Institute of Southeast Asian Studies.
1999   *The Asian Crisis Turns Global.* Singapore: Institute of Southeast Asian Studies.

— The first book deals with the economic troubles in Southeast Asia, while the second book is concerned with international repercussion of the financial disaster. (LC No. HB3722.M65 1998 and HB3808.M66 1999)

Mulder, Niels.
1992   *Inside Southeast Asia: Thai, Javanese and Filipino: Interpretations of Everyday Life.* Bangkok: Editions Duang Kamol.

— Views of social life, religion, and customs in Buddhist Thailand, Muslim Java, and Christian Philippines. Includes bibliographical references. (LC No. DS 568.M85 1992)

Muslim, Macapado Abaton.
1994   *The Moro Armed Struggle in the Philippines: The Nonviolent Autonomy Alternative.* Marawi City, Philippines: Office of the President and College of Public Affairs, Mindanao State University.

— A Maranao scholar suggests possibilities for peace between the majority Christian government and the Muslim minority in the southern Philippines. Includes bibliographical references. (LC No. DS666.M8 M86 1994)

Mutalib, Hussain.
1990   *Islam and Ethnicity in Malay Politics.* Singapore and New York: Oxford University Press.

— Concerned with how the many ethnic Malay groups influence religion and politics. Includes bibliographical references. (LC No. BP63.M27 H87 1990)

Nair, Shanti.
1997   *Islam in Malaysian Foreign Policy.* London and New York: Routledge.

— Demonstrates how Islam influences internal politics and foreign relations in Malaysia. Includes bibliographical references. (LC No. BP63.M27 N35 1997)

Neher, Clark D.
1995   *Democracy and Development in Southeast Asia: The Winds of Change.* Boulder, Colo.: Westview Press.
1998   *Southeast Asia in the New International Era.* Boulder, Colo.: Westview Press.

— Describes government and politics in Asia and the Pacific with focus on Southeast Asia. Includes bibliographical references. (LC No. JQ96.A91 N44 1995 and DS526.7.N45 1998)

Osborne, Milton E.

1997   *Southeast Asia: An Introductory History.* St. Leonard's, New South Wales, Australia: Allen & Unwin.

     — A summary history of the entire region. Includes bibliographical references. (LC No. DS525.O8 1997)

Osman, Mohd. Taib, Editor.

1997   *Islamic Civilization in the Malay World.* Kuala Lumpur, Malaysia: Dewan Bahasa dan Pustaka and the Research Centre for Islamic History, Art and Culture, Istanbul, Turkey.

     — A Muslim view of Malay Muslim civilization, economic life, law, education, mysticism, social life, and customs. Includes bibliographical references. (LC No. BP63.M27 186 1997)

Parry, William J.

1992   *An Ethnographic Bibliography for South and Southeast Asian Hunters and Gatherers.* New Haven: Human Relations Area Files.

     — Title is self-explanatory. Covers resource publications for minority groups. (LC No. Z5115.P37 1992)

Pitsuwan, Surin.

1985   *Islam and Malay Nationalism: A Case Study of Malay-Muslims of Southern Thailand.* Bangkok: Thai Khadi Research Institute, Thammasat University.

     — The little-known Muslim minority in southern Thailand and their struggles with the majority Buddhist government of Thailand. Bibliography. (LC No. DS570.M3 S87 1985)

Pongsapich, Amara, Michael C. Howard, and Jacques Amyot, Editors.

1992   *Regional Development and Change in Southeast Asia in the 1990s.* Bangkok: Chulalongkom University, Social Research Institute.

     — Gives insights into social and economic conditions influenced by regional planning and urbanization in the entire region in early 1990s. Includes bibliographical references. (LC No. HT395.A85 R44 1992)

Reid, Anthony, Editor.

1993   *Southeast Asia in the Early Modern Era.* Ithaca, N.Y.: Cornell University Press.

     — A brief history of recent events in Southeast Asia. Includes bibliographical references. (LC No. DS526.4.S68 1993)

Report on International Seminar on Islamic Civilization in the Malay World.

1989   Bandar Seri Begawan: Ministry of Religious Affairs, Negara Brunei Darussalam.

     — An authentic Malay Muslim view of Islamic civilization, history, art, and cul-

ture among Malays. Includes bibliographical references. (LC No. BP63.A4 148
1989)

Reynolds, Craig J., and Ruth Thomas McVey.
1998   *Southeast Asian Studies: Reorientations.* Ithaca, N.Y.: Cornell Southeast Asia
        Program Publications.

— Describes self-cultivation and self-determination in post-colonial Southeast
  Asia. Also discusses globalization, marginalization, and international economic relations in the Frank H. Golay Memorial lectures. (LC No. HC441.S74
  1998)

Rigg, Jonathan.
1995   *Southeast Asia.* Austin, Tex.: Raintree Steck-Vaughn.

— Examines the landscapes, climate, weather, population, culture, and indus-
  tries of Southeast Asia. Includes bibliographical references. (LC No.
  DS521.R54 1995)

Rony, Abdul Kohar, and Ieda Siqueira Wiarda.
1997   *The Portuguese in Southeast Asia: Malacca, Moluccas, East Timor.* Hamburg:
        Abera Verlag.

— History of the first European Christian colonialist penetration into the Malay Muslim world. Bibliography. (LC No. Z3221.R66 1997)

Sachsenroder, Wolfgang.
1998   *Political Party Systems and Democratic Development in East and Southeast
        Asia.* Aldershot, Hants, U.K. and Brookfield, Vt.: Ashgate.

— Perceptions of German scholars into the role of politics and government in
  the development of nations in East and Southeast Asia. (LC No. JQ750.A58
  P67 1998)

SarDesai, D. R.
1994   *Southeast Asia: Past and Present.* Boulder, Colo.: Westview Press.

— A history of entire region. Includes bibliographical references. (LC No.
  DS525.S27 1994)

Savage, Victor R., Lily Kong, and Warwick Neville, Editors.
1996   *The Naga Awakens: Growth and Change in Southeast Asia.* Singapore: Times
        Academic Press.

— The *Naga* is the mythical serpent of folktales. This is a series of papers on recent developments in Southeast Asia including the introduction of technology, computers, environmental concerns, and social development strategy.
  Includes bibliographical references. (LC No. HC441.N25 1998)

Schouten, M. J. C.
1998   *Leadership and Social Mobility in a Southeast Asian Society: Minahasa.* Leiden: KITLV.

— A revision of the author's Ph.D. Thesis at Vrije Universiteit, Amsterdam. Describes leadership, social life, and customs of people in Minahasa, Indonesia. (LC No. HN710.Z9 S657 1998)

Seminar on "Fanaticism and Islam."
1995   Kuala Lumpur, Malaysia: The International Islamic University.

— Reports on a seminar on Islamic fundamentalism organized by the Students' Representative Council with the cooperation of the Institut Kefahaman Islam Malaysia (IKIM). (LC No. Microfiche 97/51638(B) South Asia)

Shiraishi, Takashi, Editor.
1994   *Approaching Suharto's Indonesia from the Margins.* Ithaca, N.Y.: Southeast Asia Program, Cornell University.

— "Translation of contemporary Japanese scholarship on Southeast Asia," covers politics, economic conditions, used clothing industry, and peasantry in Indonesia. Includes bibliographical references. (LC No. HC447.A856 1994)

Southeast Asia: The Information Age.
1996   Washington, D.C.: Special Libraries Association.

— Proceedings of the State-of-the-Art Institute, November 2-3, 1995, Washington, D.C. Reports on information services and telecommunications industry in Southeast Asia. (LC No. HD9999.I493 A7857 1996)

Sugiyama, Shinya, and Milagros C. Guerrero, Editors.
1994   *International Commercial Rivalry in Southeast Asia in the Interwar Period.* New Haven: Yale Center for International and Area Studies.

— Presents history of commercial relation with Japan and countries of Southeast Asia. Includes bibliographical references. (LC No. HF3828.A75 I57 1994)

Sullivan, John.
1991   *Inventing and Imagining Community: Two Modern Indonesian Ideologies.* Clayton, Victoria, Australia: Centre of Southeast Asian Studies, Monash University.

— A study of citizenship, political culture, ideology, and community in Indonesia by Australian researcher. Includes bibliographical references. (LC No. JQ777.A2 S584 1991)

Suryadinata, Leo.
1989   *Military Ascendancy and Political Culture: A Study of Indonesia's Golkar.* Athens, Ohio: Ohio University, Center for International Studies.

— History of Golongan Karya (Golkar), Indonesia's dominant political organization under leadership of Sukarno and Suharto with strong influence of Armed Forces from 1950 to 1989. Bibliography. (LC No. JQ779.A576 S87 1989)

Taher, Tarmizi.
1997   *Aspiring for the Middle Path: Religious Harmony in Indonesia.* Djakarta: Center for Study of Islam and Society.

— Deals with Pancasila and relations between Islam and Christianity and government efforts to promote religious harmony. Includes bibliographical references. (LC BP63.15 T353 1997)

Tarling, Nicholas.
1998   *Nations and States in Southeast Asia.* Cambridge and New York: Cambridge University Press.

— History, historiography of the formation of nations in Southeast Asia after World War II. Includes bibliographical references. (LC No. DS526.7.T36 1998)

Taylor, John G., and Andrew Turton, Editors.
1988   *Southeast Asia.* New York: Monthly Review Press.

— Covers social conditions throughout Southeast Asia. Bibliography. (LC No. HN690.8.A8 S68 1988)

Thaib, Lukman.
1996   *Readings on the Politics and Governments of Southeast Asia.* Bangi, Malaysia: Universiti Kebangsaan Malaysia.

— Title is self-explanatory. Includes bibliographical references. (LC No. DS526.7.L8 1996)

1996   *Political Dimensions of Islam in Southeast Asia.* Bangi, Malaysia: Universiti Kebangsaan.

— The role of Islam in government and politics in Southeast Asia. Also deals with Islamic fundamentalism. Includes bibliographical references. (LC No. BP173.7.L85 1996)

Tibi, Bassam.
1998   *The Challenge of Fundamentalism: Political Islam and the New World Disorder.* Berkeley: University of California Press.

— The role and challenge of Islamic fundamentalism in religion and politics throughout the world in the latter part of the twentieth century. Includes bibliographical references. (LC No. BP173.7.T56 1998)

Trocki, Carl A., Editor.

1998   *Gangsters, Democracy and the State in Southeast Asia.* Ithaca, N.Y.: Cornell University Press.

— Describes how governments deal with criminals in Southeast Asia. Includes bibliographical references. (LC No. DS526.7.G36 1998)

Van Esterik, Penny, Editor.

1996   *Women of Southeast Asia.* DeKalb: Northern Illinois University, Center for Southeast Asian Studies.

— Describes the role of women in various countries of Southeast Asia. Includes bibliographical references. (LC No. HQ1745.8.W65 1996)

Von der Mehden, Fred R.

1993   *Two Worlds of Islam: Interaction Between Southeast Asia and the Middle East.* Gainesville: University of Florida Press.

— Explains relationships and distinctions between Malay and Arab Muslims. Includes bibliographical references. (LC No. DS525.9.M628 V66 1993)

Wicks, Peter.

1991   *Literary Perspectives on Southeast Asia: Collected Essays.* Toowoomba, Australia: University of South Queensland Press.

— History and criticism of folktales and other literature. (LC No. PL3508.05.W5 1991)

Winzeler, Robert L., Editor.

1997   *Indigenous Peoples and the State: Politics, Land, and Ethnicity in the Malayan Peninsula and Borneo.* New Haven: Yale University Southeast Asia Studies.

— Reports on several minority ethnic tribal groups, their culture, religion, and relationships in the Malayan Peninsula and Borneo. (LC No. GN635.M4 163 1997)

Wurfel, David, and Bruce Burton, Editors.

1990   *The Political Economy of Foreign Policy in Southeast Asia.* New York: St. Martin's Press.

— Revision of papers presented at the conference on "Managing of the External Environment: The Political Economy of Foreign Policy in Southeast Asia" held at University of Windsor in June, 1987. Includes case studies of International Division of Labor and foreign economic relations. Includes bibliographical references. (LC No. HF1591.P65 1990)

1996   *Southeast Asia in the New World Order: The Political Economy of a Dynamic Region.* New York: St. Martin's Press.

— A study of economic development in the entire region just before the economic collapse and crisis in the late 1990s. (LC No. HF5549.5.M3 T67 1994)

Yates, Maria, and Richard.
1994   *Malaysia, No Problem Lah!: Four Years in Malaysia and Southeast Asia.* Parsons, W. Va.: McClain Printing Co.

— A diary with Western view of travel and life during four years in Southeast Asia, with emphasis on Malaysia. (LC No. DS592.6.Y38 1994)

Index